S0-BCN-855

Property of
Saint Mary School
Bethel, CT

TECHNOLOGY

in the

20th
century

Copyright © 1997 Bluewood Books

All rights reseved. No part of this publication may be reproduced, stored in a retrieval system or transmitted in any form by any means, electronic, mechanical, photocopying or otherwise, without first obtaining written permission of the copyright owner.

This edition produced and published in 1997 by Bluewood Books A Division of The Siyeh Group, Inc., P.O. Box 689 San Mateo, CA 94401

ISBN 0-912517-25-5

Printed in USA
10, 9, 8, 7, 6, 5, 4, 3, 2, 1

Designed by Linda Wanczyk
Production by Eric Irving
Copy Edited by J. Bonasia
Edited by Richard Michaels and
Barbara Krystal
Proofread by Robert Juran

About the Author:
Alex Chase is a freelance writer, editor and proofreader. Born in the Ukranian city of Uzhgorod, he moved to Los Angeles at the age of four. He earned a B.A. in English from the University of California at Santa Barbara and now lives in San Francisco.

The publisher wishes to thank and acknowledge the following for the courtesy of reproducing the following images:
Apple Computers, Inc. 143(b), 144; Archive Photos 112; Archive Photos/AFP 106; Archive Photos/Express Newspapers 37, 67; Argonne National Laboratory 174; Army Communication Museum 51, 107, 132; Army Ordnance Museum 65, 101; Property of AT&T. Reprinted with permission 103,131, 135, 146; Bakelite Corporation 41, 42(t); Boeing Company 56, 84, 113, 125, 161, 164; Carillon Historical Park 48; Chevron Corporation 73, 75, 76, 141, 170; DuPont Nylon Company 87; Eastern National/Wright Brothers National Museum 34; Edison Ford Winter Estates 31, 45; Enrico Fermi Institute 96; Ford Motor Company 47; General Dynamics Company/Electric Boat Corporation 115; Historical Electronics Museum 83; IBM Corporation 4, 81,102,104,139; Intel Corporation 142, 172; Lawrence Berkeley Livermore Laboratory/U.S. Dept.of Energy 77; Library of Congress 32, 33; Matag Corporation 44; Microsoft Corporation 143(t), 157, 158, 170(t); NASA 6, 74, 114, 123, 127, 128, 129, 147, 148, 149, 153, 162; National Archives 46, 4 53, 91, 93, 95, 97; NCR Corporation 35; Copyright 1996 Netscape Communications Corp. Used with permission. All Rights Reserved 170(b), 171; PARC Xerox Corporation 144, 156; Philadelphi College of Textiles and Science/Pal Design Institute 54; Post Street Archives/Dow Chemical Company 42(b); Radio Corporation of Americ 39, 80; San Diego Aerospace Museum 52; 3M Company 69; Tex Instruments Incorporated 116, 119, 120, 136; Technology Museum of Innovation 167, 176; Unisys 118; U.S. Postal Service 68, 89, 160; U.S. Submarine Force Museum 59; United Technologies 86; Jerry Vanicek 40; Westinghouse Electric Corporation 82; Xerox Corporatio 90; Zenith Electronics Corporation 121.

TABLE OF CONTENTS

Technology is the main driving force behind human history; it is how we define ourselves. We are not the only animals to use tools: Beavers build dams, otters break open shells with rocks, and birds use twigs to reach their insect prey hiding in trees. Humans, however, are the only animals to manufacture the tools they use. In the study of human evolution, scientists consider Homo habilis ("handy man") to be the first human species, because about two million years ago these creatures became the first to make tools. Earlier human ancestors used bones, rocks, and sticks as tools, but there is no evidence of their modifying these objects to better fit their needs.

Since that time, humans have evolved into Homo sapiens ("rational man"). Our tools have become more advanced, and we have populated much of the earth's land regardless of terrain or climate. Technology has allowed humans to make their homes in diverse areas from deserts and jungles to frozen tundras and remote islands in the far reaches of the oceans. Prehistoric people learned to use technology to cultivate the land and grow food rather than having to constantly hunt for it in the wild. Agricultural societies soon grew, evolved into cities, and civilization was born. With large groups of people living close together, an environment conducive to the interchange of ideas fostered accelerated technological development. Many innovations followed over the centuries. A fundamental shift in technological development came in the early 18th century when humans learned to generate energy by burning coal and eventually other fossil fuels such as oil and natural gas. The result was the Industrial Revolution, which began in England and quickly spread to other parts of the world, especially Western Europe and the United States. Still, technology's effect on the daily life of the average person of the 18th century was not as dramatic as what was to come.

As the 19th century was coming to a close, many innovations began to be introduced that would have a profound social, political, and economic impact on the industrialized world. It was a world dominated by mechanical technology, but electrical engineering was becoming the next great

IBM Integrated circuit chip, 1969

technological frontier. Electricity provided a new and increasingly essential form of energy. The telephone, the electric light bulb, and the automobile had been invented by this time, and while they may not yet have been widely used, these devices would soon contribute to the transformation of the planet.

The Earth and people's perceptions about it were also beginning to change. In 1890, the United States Census Bureau announced the end of the nation's unexplored frontier. With major advances in transportation and communication, our once vast world suddenly appeared to be shrinking. Revolutionary developments in these two areas during the 20th century would perpetuate this perception, and humans would become more dependent on technology than ever before.

At the turn of the century, few people ever dreamed that within the next hundred years — or ever — humans would walk on the moon, create weapons of mass destruction utilizing the smallest units of matter, or journey through a limitless and intangible world called cyberspace made up entirely of binary digits called zeroes and ones.

Technology of the 20th century affects the lives of virtually everyone on the planet — from inhabitants of the largest cities in the industrialized world to indigenous peoples in the heart of the rain forest. Technology has given us the power to alter the environment to fit our needs. All of these advances, however, do not come without some cost. During the 20th century, humans began to learn that the obvious benefits of certain technologies can have less evident and highly detrimental side effects.

Today, we must carefully weigh both the benefits and risk factors (long and short range) in order to justify technology. As technology continues to progress, the justification process will become more complex and crucial.

Many of the most important and far-reaching inventions were not recognized as such at the time of their introduction. These innovations were often the products of visionary thinkers who persevered through repeated difficulties. With new approaches, past failures were not omens of future disappointments, but harbingers of eventual success. Some exciting and revolutionary discoveries cropped up out of unrelated research; others originated out of necessity and desperation, especially during times of war.

The purpose of this book is to present a historical overview of technology in the 20th century. A chronology of technological milestones traces the steps that have been taken over the past 100 years. The text is divided into ten chapters, each presenting the major advances of the decade. Since the history of technology is so intimately intertwined with the history of humanity, an introductory section in each chapter sets the historical context of the decade discussed.

Turning back the clock to January 1, 1900, we will explore how technology has dramatically changed the world and the way we live in it — from groundbreaking developments such as the atomic bomb and landing humans on the moon to purely recreational items like CDs and Silly Putty. Whether monumental or seemingly frivolous, every one of these innovations was born out of a human need, for as the great Greek philosopher Plato said 2,400 years ago, "The true creator is necessity, which is the mother of our invention."

Apollo 15 mission uses first Lunar Roving Vehicle

TECHNOLOGY

chronology

of the

20th century

1900-1909

1900

Mar 24 Construction begins on the first tunnel of New York's subterranean rapid transit system.

Apr 14 The first public escalator is introduced at the opening of the World Exposition in Paris. It is designed by Charles D. Seeberger and built by the Otis Elevator Company.

July 2 Count Ferdinand von Zeppelin launches his first rigid, hydrogen filled airship in Germany.

Dec 14 Max Planck announces his quantum theory of relativity, which states that radiation is transmitted in small units.

◆ Johann Waaler patents the paper clip.

◆ The Packard Model C becomes the first car with a steering wheel.

1901

Oct 24 The Eastman Kodak Company introduces the Brownie camera. The easy-to-use camera sells for one dollar.

Dec 12 Guglielmo Marconi sends the first trans-Atlantic radio transmission from England to Newfoundland, Canada.

◆ Reginald Aubrey Fessenden invents the high-frequency alternator, allowing for continuous radio waves, which makes the transmission of audio signals possible.

◆ General Electric becomes the first U.S. company to open a research laboratory.

◆ The Merry Oldsmobile becomes the first car with a speedometer. It is also the first mass-produced automobile in the U.S.

◆ Blickensderfer Electric manufactures the first electric typewriter.

1902

Oct 17 Cadillac sells its first car.

◆ Hubert Cecil Booth invents the vacuum cleaner.

◆ Willis H. Carrier invents the air conditioner.

◆ Edwin Binney makes Crayola crayons by combining paraffin, oil, and stearic acid with assorted pigments.

◆ Arthur Little, William Walker, and Harry Mork patent rayon, the first synthetic fiber.

1903

May 23 The first telephone connection between Paris and Rome becomes operational.

July 23 Ford sells its first car, the Model A.

Nov 3 William Einthoven invents the electrocardiograph (EKG), a device to monitor the electric currents of the heart and detect potential abnormalities.

Dec 17 Orville and Wilbur Wright become the first people to achieve free flight in a heavier-than-air craft at Kitty Hawk, North Carolina.

♦ Konstantin Tsiolkovsky publishes *Research into Interplanetary Space by Means of Rocket Power* in which he advocates the use of liquid-propelled rockets for space travel as well as other principles later adopted and used in space flights.

1904

Mar 22 London *Daily Illustrated Mirror* publishes the first color photograph.

July 31 The 4,607-mile Trans-Siberian Railroad is completed in Russia. Construction began in 1891 on the railway connecting the Ural Mountains with Russia's Pacific coast.

Oct 27 New York City's underground railway, the Interborough Rapid Transit (IRT), opens after a day of celebration. It is the most extensive subway system in the world.

Nov 18 The U.S. signs a treaty with Panama to build a canal connecting the Pacific and Atlantic Oceans through the Isthmus of Panama.

♦ John Ambrose Fleming invents and patents the vacuum tube. Also called the Fleming valve, the thermionic valve, and diode, it uses heat to regulate electric current flow in one direction.

♦ Leon Guillet produces the first stainless steel, but he does not recognize its non-corrosive properties.

1905

Mar 17 Albert Einstein publishes a paper on the light-quantum theory. It explains the photoelectric effect by which certain metals release electrons when exposed to light.

Apr 1 The first telephone connection between Paris and Berlin becomes operational.

June 30 Albert Einstein publishes his Special Theory of Relativity, which includes the famous equation $E=mc^2$. The theory provides much of the basis for the subsequent research and development of atomic energy.

July 8 In St. Louis, Missouri, the American Gasoline Company opens the first drive-in gas station.

♦ Guglielmo Marconi invents the directional radio antenna.

♦ General Electric introduces the tungsten filament light bulb, which has a longer lifespan than carbon filaments.

1906

May 22 The Wright Brothers patent their aircraft design.

Oct 17 Arthur Korn transmits the first photographs through telegraph lines and calls the process telephotography.

Nov 25 Lee de Forest invents the triode vacuum tube, a better electrical amplifier than Fleming's diode and the basis for most electronics in the first half of the century.

Dec 24   Reginald Aubrey Fessenden transmits the first audio broadcast using radio waves.

1907

June 10   Auguste and Louis Lumiere devise a practical color photography process.

July 14   Leo Baekeland patents Bakelite, the first synthetic plastic.

Nov 13   Paul Cornu makes the first flight in a helicopter, but he only rises one foot off the ground and remains airborne for 20 seconds.

◆   Hans Geiger invents a radioactivity-measuring device called a Geiger counter.

1908

Feb 10   The U.S. signs a contract with the Wright Brothers to purchase its first military airplane.

Oct 1   Ford Motor Company introduces the Model T, a car that remains in production until 1927.

Nov 22   The U.S. Postal Service purchases automobiles to assist in mail delivery.

Dec 1   Heike Kammerling Onnes liquefies helium to achieve extremely low temperatures approaching absolute zero.

◆   Cadillac becomes the first company to use interchangeable parts in automobile manufacturing.

◆   Jacques Brandenberger invents cellophane.

◆   Frederick Cottrell patents an electrostatic precipitator to reduce air pollution by removing dust, ash, and other particles from the emissions of industrial smoke stacks.

1909

June 25   Louis Blériot becomes the first person to cross the English Channel in a heavier-than-air craft.

◆   General Electric begins manufacturing the first electric toaster.

◆   Georges Claude invents neon lighting.

1910-1919

1910

Mar 28   Henri Fabre flies the first seaplane.

June 2   Charles Rolls completes the first round-trip airplane flight over the English Channel.

Oct 16   Count Ferdinand von Zeppelin starts the German Airship Transport Company (DELAG), the first commercial airline company.

Nov 14   Eugene Ely demonstrates the concept of the aircraft carrier by becoming the first pilot to take off from the deck of a ship in an airplane.

1911

Jan	18	Eugene Ely becomes the first pilot to land an airplane on a ship.
Apr	12	Pierre Prier completes the first non-stop flight from London to Paris.
July	11	Charles Kettering invents the first practical self-starter for automobiles to replace the crank shaft.
Oct	22	The Italian Army becomes the first to use airplanes for military purposes in its war with the Ottoman Turks.
◆		Isaac Newton Lewis develops a lightweight machine gun.
◆		Heike Kamerlingh Onnes discovers superconductivity, the ability of metals to conduct electricity without resistance at extremely low temperatures.

1912

Jan	10	The first practical seaplane, designed by Glenn Curtiss, makes its maiden flight.
Apr	10	A radio transmission from London becomes the first to be received by an aircraft.
Apr	14	The luxury liner Titanic runs into an iceberg and sinks on its maiden voyage. It also becomes the first ship to send wireless distress signals.
Sep	9	J. Vedriens becomes the first pilot to fly faster than 100 miles per hour, reaching speeds of up to 107 miles per hour.
Sep	22	Edwin Howard Armstrong invents the regenerative circuit, which improves the reception and amplification of the triode vacuum tube.
◆		Corona manufactures a portable typewriter.
◆		Garrett Morgan invents the gas mask, which he calls the safety hood.

1913

Jan	7	William Burton of Standard Oil patents thermal cracking, a refining process for converting oil into gasoline.
May	13	Igor Sikorsky flies the Bolshoi, the first airplane with four engines.
Oct	7	Ford Motor Company begins using a moving assembly line to mass produce automobiles.
Nov	5	The aqueduct from Owens Valley to Los Angeles begins operation.
Dec	19	Gideon Sundback develops the first practical and commercially successful hook fastener which becomes known as the zipper.
◆		Irving Langmuir develops a longer-lasting light bulb by filling it with an inert gas that makes the tungsten filament evaporate more slowly.

1914

Aug	5	The first electric traffic signals begin operating in Cleveland, Ohio with red and green lights to control the flow of automobile traffic.
Aug	15	The Panama Canal opens.
Sep	22	German U-boats demonstrate the submarine's effectiveness by sinking three British armored cruisers within one hour.

Dec 21   A German aircraft becomes the first to drop an aerial bomb.

◆   The Boston Wire Stretcher Company begins marketing the first desk model staplers.

1915

Jan 19   German Zeppelins begin to bomb England.

Jan 25   Alexander Graham Bell talks to colleague Thomas Watson in the first trans-continental telephone call from New York to San Francisco.

Apr 1   French pilot Roland Garros becomes the first to shoot down another airplane with a front-mounted machine gun. Raymond Saulnier installed metal deflectors on the airplane's propeller to protect it from the machine gun's fire.

Apr 22   Germany's chlorine gas attack at Ypres, Belgium is the first use of poison gas in warfare. The chemical is developed by Fritz Haber.

June 6   A British airplane shoots down a Zeppelin bomber over England for the first time.

July 1   German airplanes first appear in battle which use a system devised by Anthony Fokker to synchronize the rotation of the propeller with the firing of the machine gun.

Dec 12   The J1 Junkers all-metal monoplane flies for the first time. It is also the first plane to use cantilevered wings, which are directly supported by the fuselage without external braces or wires.

Dec 19   Albert Einstein postulates his new theory of relativity.

◆   Manson Benedicks discovers the semiconductive properties of germanium crystals.

◆   Corning Glass Works develops Pyrex, a heat-resistant glass used in cookware.

◆   Paul Langevin invents sonar as a way for ships to detect icebergs.

1916

Sep 15   The British introduce the tank as a weapon of war at the Battle of the Somme. The tanks, however, are not used effectively at this time.

◆   Joel Fisher develops the modern washing machine.

1917

Oct 19   Germany makes its last Zeppelin bombing raid and airplanes begin to take over as more effective bombers.

Nov 20   The British use tanks successfully for the first time at the Battle of Cambrai.

◆   Edwin Howard Armstrong invents the superheterodyne circuit, which simplifies radio operation.

◆   Albert Einstein postulates the theory of stimulated emissions, which later becomes instrumental in the development of the laser.

1918

May 15   The U.S. Army initiates the first airmail service.

June 27   A parachute is used for the first time.

Oct 12   The U.S. Post Office takes over operation of airmail service.

◆   The Kelvinator mechanical refrigerator becomes the first commercially successful model for home use.

1919

June 14   John Alcock and Arthur Whitten-Brown make the first non-stop aerial crossing of the Atlantic Ocean by flying from Newfoundland, Canada to Ireland.

July 13   The British airship R34 completes the first trans-Atlantic round-trip flight.

Aug 25   Aircraft Transport and Travel begins commercial passenger service between Paris and London.

◆   Hugo Koch invents the Enigma encoding machine, later used by Germany during World War II.

◆   Robert Watson-Watt patents the concept of echolocation, which uses radio waves to locate airborne planes.

1920-1929

1920

Nov 2   Radio station KDKA in Pittsburgh makes the first scheduled commercial broadcast with coverage of the U.S. presidential election.

◆   Robert Goddard publishes *A Method of Reaching Extreme Altitudes* in which he proposed the use of liquid fuel rockets to escape Earth's gravity.

◆   John Thompson patents the submachine gun which becomes famous as the Tommy Gun.

1921

Jan 19   The British airship R34 crashes and kills 40 people.

Jan 25   The first performance of the play R.U.R. in which author Karel Capek coins the term robot (derived from "robota," the Czech word for worker) to describe his artificial human characters.

Feb 22   The U.S. Post office initiates airmail service between New York and San Francisco.

◆   Thomas Midgley and T. A. Boyd discover that a small amount of lead added to a car's gasoline prevents knock. It is later discovered that lead additives in gasoline cause severe environmental pollution.

◆   The German Avus Autobahn is completed. It is the first highway, a road allowing the free flow of traffic by eliminating intersections.

1922

Apr 21   Lee de Forest announces his invention of Phonofilm, a system of recording audio tracks directly onto motion picture film.

Aug 28   The first radio commercial airs on WEAF in New York City.

1923

Nov 20   Garret Morgan patents his three-way traffic signal, which introduces the yellow caution light.

Nov 25   Trans-Atlantic radio broadcasting between the U.S. and England begins.

◆   Vladimir Zworykin applies for a patent for the iconoscope, an electronic television camera.

1924

Feb 8   The gas chamber is used for an execution in the U.S. for the first time.

May 12   The Brooklyn Edison Company begins operating the world's largest steam generator.

◆   Zenith manufactures the first commercial portable radio.

◆   John Logie Baird transmits the first image using his mechanical television system.

◆   Vladimir Zworykin applies for a patent for the kinescope, an electronic television receiver using a cathode-ray tube (CRT).

◆   A network of flashing beacons are installed on the ground along airmail flight paths in the U.S. to help pilots with navigation.

1925

June 20   Herr Schaetzle demonstrates a wireless car phone in Berlin.

July 9   New York City tests its air for carbon monoxide, a poisonous gas emitted by automobiles.

◆   Richard Drew of the Minnesota Mining and Manufacturing Company (now called 3M) invents Scotch tape.

◆   The Bronx River Parkway opens. It is the first freeway in the U.S.

1926

Jan 27   John Logie Baird demonstrates his mechanical television system to the Royal Society of London.

Mar 16   Robert Goddard launches the first liquid fuel rocket.

Feb 26   Long distance telephone service between San Francisco and London is established.

1927

May 21   Charles Lindbergh becomes the first person to fly non-stop from New York to Paris.

Sep	8	John Logie Baird transmits mechanical television images from Leeds to London.
Oct	6	*The Jazz Singer*, a movie starring Al Jolsen, ushers in the era of talking motion pictures, also called talkies.
Oct	14	Oil is discovered in Northern Iraq, an event that gradually leads to the Middle East's development as the world's most important oil producing region.
◆		Philo Farnsworth develops the image dissector, an electronic television system.
◆		Harold Stephen Black develops the negative feedback amplifier to reduce distortion in radio and telephone equipment.

1928

Jan	13	General Electric transmits experimental television broadcasts in New York.
Feb	8	John Logie Baird transmits the first trans-Atlantic television broadcast from London to New York.
June	11	Fritz Stamer makes the first manned flight by rocket propulsion.
Oct	12	The iron lung, a mechanical respiration device invented by Philip Dinker & Louis Shaw in 1927, is used commercially for the first time.
◆		Jacob Schick patents the first commercially successful electric razor.
◆		Edwin Land develops a polarized light filter for cameras.

1929

Jan	7	Sheffield Farms in New York begins to package milk in wax paper boxes instead of glass bottles.
June	27	Bell Labs demonstrates a high-resolution color television system.
Sep	24	U.S. Army pilot James Doolittle performs the first flight using only instruments for navigation.
Sep	30	The British Broadcasting Corporation (BBC) begins experimental broadcast of John Logie Baird's mechanical television system.

1930-1939

1930

Apr	17	Wallace Hume Carothers creates a synthetic rubber called Neoprene.
May	13	Airmail service between Paris and Brazil begins.
June	7	Construction of Boulder Dam begins.
◆		I. G. Farben Corporation develops a magnetic tape recorder.
◆		Thomas Midgley develops the refrigerant freon, the first commercial chlorofluorocarbon (CFC).
◆		Philo Farnsworth patents the image dissector.
◆		Vannevar Bush builds the differential analyzer computer.
◆		Frank Whittle patents a design for a jet engine.

1931

July	1	Trans-Africa railway opens.
July	1	Wiley Post and Harold Gatty land in New York and complete the first round-the-world flight.
July	31	Ernest O. Lawrence invents the cyclotron, a kind of atomic particle accelerator.
Aug	8	The Goodyear Corporation builds a 785-foot long airship for the U.S. Navy.
Oct	24	The George Washington Bridge opens in New York City under budget and eight months ahead of schedule. It spans 3,500 feet across the Hudson River.
Nov	19	RCA Victor releases the first long-playing (LP) record, but it cannot find commercial success in the poor economy of the Great Depression.

1932

Feb	27	James Chadwick announces his discovery of the neutron.
May	21	Amelia Earhart becomes the first woman to make an aerial crossing of the Atlantic by flying from Newfoundland to Ireland. She also set a record for the fastest trans-Atlantic crossing time.
Dec	23	Telephone service between Hawaii and the U.S. begins.
◆		Electric and Musical Industries (EMI) patents the Emitron, an electronic television camera that the BBC later adopts for its broadcasts.

1933

Mar	12	American President Franklin D. Roosevelt makes the first radio broadcast of his series of fireside chats.
June	6	The first drive-in movie theater opens in Camden, New Jersey.
June	22	The Illinois waterway opens, providing a shipping link between the Great Lakes and the Gulf of Mexico.
July	22	Wiley Post completes the first solo flight around the world.
Dec	6	Edwin Howard Armstrong receives the first of five patents for frequency modulation (FM), a quieter form of radio transmission than amplitude modulation (AM).
◆		Walther Meissner and Robert Ochsenfield discover the Meissner effect, a superconductor's ability to repel magnets.
◆		Ernst Ruska builds the first electron microscope, which produces much greater amplification than light microscopes.
◆		RCA demonstrates its electronic television system in an experimental broadcast.

1934

Mar	12	Leo Szilard patents a design for an atomic bomb.
Dec	19	Wernher von Braun and his colleagues launch Germany's first liquid fuel rockets.
◆		Wallace Hume Carothers and his colleagues at Du Pont invent nylon.

1935

Feb 26 Robert Watson-Watt successfully tests his radar system by detecting a flying airplane.

Apr 16 Pan American Airways initiates air service to the Orient from San Francisco.

◆ Gibson guitar company begins to manufacture electric guitars.

◆ Vannevar Bush builds an improved differential analyzer computer.

◆ Hans von Ohain patents a design for a jet engine.

1936

Feb 26 The Volkswagen, or people's car, begins its production run, which becomes the greatest in automotive history in 1972 when it breaks the record set by Ford's Model T.

Dec 17 The Douglas DC-3 flies for the first time. It is the first reliable transport plane and revolutionizes the airline industry.

◆ The BBC begins transmitting the first regular daily television broadcasts.

1937

Apr 12 Frank Whittle successfully bench tests the first aircraft jet engine.

May 6 The Zeppelin Hindenburg, the largest dirigible ever built, explodes over Lakehurst, New Jersey, and the era of airship transport comes to an end. The event is also covered in the first coast-to-coast radio broadcast.

May 27 The Golden Gate Bridge in San Francisco is completed and becomes the world's longest suspension bridge.

July 2 Amelia Earhart and Frederick Noonan disappear over the Pacific Ocean in an attempted round-the-world flight.

1938

Apr 6 Roy J. Plunkett of Du Pont accidentally invents teflon.

Oct 22 Chester Carlson makes the first photocopy using a process called xerography, which means dry writing in Greek.

Dec 17 Otto Hahn becomes the first to achieve nuclear fission, the splitting of an atom.

◆ The brothers Ladislao and George Biro invent the ballpoint pen.

1939

Aug 2 A letter signed by renowned international scientists urges President Franklin D. Roosevelt to develop an atomic weapon before Nazi Germany can do so.

Aug 27 A Heinkel He 178 becomes the first jet-powered aircraft to fly. It is powered by an engine designed by Hans von Ohain.

Sep 14 Igor Sikorsky successfully flies the VS-300, which becomes the first commercially successful helicopter. Its configuration becomes the most commonly used in helicopter design.

Oct 19 — RCA agrees to pay Philo Farnsworth royalties for his electronic television system.

◆ John Turon Randall and Henry Albert Boot invent the multicavity magnetron, a microwave transmitting device that makes radar effective in any weather and using smaller antennae.

◆ Paul Müller invents the pesticide DDT.

1940-1949

1940

July 10 — The British Royal Air Force (RAF) first uses radar in combat to repel the invading Germans in the Battle of Britain.

Sep 11 — George Stibitz and Samuel Williams remotely operate a computer in New York from Dartmouth University in New Hampshire.

Oct 1 — The Pennsylvania Turnpike opens and becomes the first modern highway in the U.S.

1941

May 15 — Frank Whittle's jet engine makes its first flight in a Gloster E28/39 airplane.

Dec 6 — President Franklin D. Roosevelt initiates the Manhattan Project to develop atomic weapons.

Dec 7 — The Japanese Navy attacks the American Pacific Fleet in Pearl Harbor, Hawaii. It is the first significant use of aircraft carriers in combat.

◆ The American rocket launcher, known as the bazooka, is developed.

1942

May 4 — The Battle of the Coral Sea is the first naval engagement in which all the fighting is conducted by carrier-based aircraft.

Oct 3 — Wernher von Braun launches the A4 rocket in the first successful flight of a guided missile. The A4 was later renamed V-2.

Dec 2 — Enrico Fermi and his team create the first man-made, self-sustaining nuclear reaction.

◆ While with the French Resistance, Jacques Yves Cousteau and Emil Gagnan invent the aqualung, also known as scuba gear.

◆ American chemists at Harvard University develop an incendiary substance called napalm.

1943

Dec 19 — Alan Turing completes the Colossus computer to decipher German codes generated by Enigma machines.

◆ James Wright accidentally invents Silly Putty.

◆ John Atanasoff and Clifford Berry build ABC, an electronic calculator.

1944

June	13	Germany begins its V-1 flying bomb attacks on London.
July	12	The British Gloster Meteor becomes the first jet fighter to enter combat service.
July	20	The German Messerschmidtt Me 262 jet fighter enters combat service.
Aug	7	Howard Aiken and colleagues complete the Harvard Mark I computer.
Sep	7	Germany begins its V-2 rocket attacks on London.

1945

June	30	John von Neumann completes a report describing the stored-program computer. His principles become the basis for future computer development.
July	12	The U.S. detonates the first atomic bomb at Alamagordo, New Mexico.
Aug	6	An American B-29 bomber nicknamed the Enola Gay dropped the atomic bomb Little Boy over the Japanese city of Hiroshima. It is the first use of a nuclear weapon in warfare.
Aug	9	The U.S. drops the atomic bomb Fat Man on the Japanese city of Nagasaki. The second nuclear attack prompts Japan to surrender and brings an end to World War II.
Oct	19	Arthur C. Clarke publishes the magazine article "Extra-Terrestrial Relays" in which he introduces the concept of geosynchronous communication satellites.
◆		Percy LeBaron Spencer invents the microwave oven, a device that heats food with the same microwaves used in radar.

1946

Feb	16	John Presper Eckert and John Mauchly demonstrate the ENIAC electronic computer.
May	12	AT&T begins to manufacture car phones.

1947

Oct	14	Chuck Yeager becomes the first person to fly faster than the speed of sound.
Dec	23	William Shockley, John Bardeen, and Walter Brattain invent the transistor.

1948

June	19	Columbia Records announces the development of the modern long-playing (LP) record by Peter Goldmark and William Bachman.

1949

Mar	2	Captain James Gallagher and his crew complete the first non-stop, round the world flight.
July	27	The de Havilland Comet, the first jet airliner, is test-flown.
Aug	29	The U.S.S.R. detonates its first atomic bomb.
◆		The Xerox Model A becomes the first photocopier to be marketed.
◆		RCA introduces the 7-inch, 45 rpm record known as the single.

1950-1959

1950

◆ John Presper Eckert and John Mauchly complete EDVAC, the first computer to employ John von Neumann's principles and Boolean logic.

1951

Jan 1 Zenith Phonevision Service in Chicago becomes the first cable television service. It transmits television signals through telephone lines, but thicker coaxial cables later become the industry standard.

June 14 John Presper Eckert and John Mauchly demonstrate UNIVAC 1, the first commercially available electronic computer. It is also the first computer to use magnetic tape for storage.

June 25 The Columbia Broadcasting System (CBS) transmits the first commercial color television broadcast using a system developed by Peter Goldmark.

Dec 1 Electricity is generated from atomic energy for the first time at the Idaho Falls testing station.

1952

May 2 De Havilland unveils the Comet jet airliner to the public. Several of the planes disappear after going into service, and all Comets are grounded in 1954 when a design flaw is discovered to be the cause of the crashes.

Nov 1 The U.S. detonates the first hydrogen bomb at Eniwetock Atoll in the Pacific Ocean. The thermonuclear bomb operates under the principles of nuclear fusion and is capable of much more powerful explosions than nuclear fission weapons.

Nov 4 UNIVAC becomes famous by predicting the outcome of the U.S. presidential election on national television.

Dec 19 International Business Machines (IBM) introduces the 701 Defense Calculator, computer developed by Bob Overton Evans.

1953

Aug 12 The U.S.S.R. detonates its first hydrogen bomb.

Aug 20 The U.S. Army tests the Redstone ballistic missile, which is later modified for space flight as the Juno rocket.

Dec 17 The Federal Communications Commission (FCC) adopts RCA's color television system as the national standard.

◆ Charles Hard Townes invents the maser.

1954

May 10 Texas Instruments introduces a transistor developed by Gordon Teal that use the semiconductor silicon instead of the more expensive germanium.

June 19 The U.S.S.R. begins operating the first nuclear power plant for civilian use.

July 15   A prototype of the Boeing 707 flies for the first time. The 707 becomes the first successful jet airliner.

Dec 10   George Devol applies for the first robotics patent.

Dec 19   Regency Electronics introduces the TR-1, the first transistor radio.

◆   Daryl Chapin, Gerald Pearson, and Calvin Fuller of AT&T's Bell Laboratories develop a semiconductor solar cell to transform sunlight into electricity.

1955

Jan 17   The U.S.S. Nautilus, the first nuclear-powered submarine, embarks on its maiden voyage.

◆   George de Mestral patents Velcro.

◆   Dr. Narinder S. Kapany invents the optical fiber.

1956

Sep 25   The first trans-Atlantic telephone cable begins operation.

1957

Aug 19   The U.S.S.R. launches the first intercontinental ballistic missile (ICBM).

Oct 4   The U.S.S.R. launches Sputnik, the first man-made object in space.

Nov 3   The U.S.S.R. launches Sputnik 2 containing the dog Laika, the first terrestrial creature to travel into space. Laika died when the air in the capsule ran out one week later.

Nov 19   Gordon Gould coins the term laser (Light Amplification by Stimulated Emission of Radiation) and devises a plan for its construction.

Dec 17   The U.S. launches an Atlas missile, its first ICBM.

Dec 18   The Shippingport reactor near Pittsburgh begins operating and becomes the first commercial nuclear power plant in the U.S.

◆   International Telephone and Telegraph (ITT) Laboratories develop the atomic clock, the world's most accurate time-keeping device.

1958

Jan 31   A Juno rocket launches Explorer 1, the first American satellite, into orbit.

Mar 15   The U.S.S.R. launches Sputnik 3 into orbit.

Mar 17   The U.S. launches Vanguard 1 into orbit. It is the first satellite to employ solar cells as a source of electricity.

Sep 12   Jack Kilby of Texas Instruments invents the integrated circuit, a device containing all the components of a circuit on a semiconductor chip.

Oct 1   The U.S. creates the National Aeronautics and Space Administration (NASA) as a civilian organization in charge of the space program.

◆   Willy Higinbotham creates the first video game.

◆   Bill Richards and his son Mark invent the skateboard.

1959

Jan	2	The U.S.S.R. launches Luna I towards the moon, but it misses its mark and goes into solar orbit.
Jan	23	Unaware of Jack Kilby's work, Robert Noyce also invents the integrated circuit and devises a way to construct it without wires.
Jan	25	American Airlines initiates the first coast-to-coast jet airline service in the U.S.
Sep	12	The U.S.S.R. launches Luna 2, and it becomes the first man-made object to reach an extra-terrestrial world by landing on the moon.
Oct	4	The U.S.S.R. launches Luna 3, which transmits images of the dark side of the moon back to Earth.
◆		Charles Hard Townes and Arthur L. Schawlow patent a design for a laser using potassium vapor as a magnifying medium.

1960-1969

1960

Apr	1	The U.S. launches TIROS I, the first weather satellite.
May	15	Theodore Maiman tests the first working laser using solid ruby as the amplifying medium.
Aug	13	The U.S. launches Echo I, a passive reflector communication satellite, into orbit.
Aug	19	The U.S.S.R. launches Sputnik 5. Equipped with a heat shield, it becomes the first spacecraft to be successfully recovered from orbit.
◆		A Xerox copier is introduced that uses toner, allowing it to operate with ordinary paper.
◆		Kenneth Olsen of Digital Equipment Corporation develops the PDP-1, the first commercial computer with a keyboard and monitor.

1961

Apr	12	The U.S.S.R. launches Vostok I into orbit and cosmonaut Yuri Gagarin becomes the first person to travel into space.
May	5	Mercury astronaut Alan Shepard becomes the first American in space, but he does not achieve orbit.
May	25	American President John F. Kennedy directs NASA to commit itself to landing man on the moon before the end of the decade.

1962

Feb	20	Mercury astronaut John Glenn becomes the first American in orbit.
July	10	NASA and Bell Labs launch Telstar I, the first commercial communications satellite, into orbit. The satellite begins broadcasting trans-Atlantic television signals the same day.
Aug	26	The U.S. launches Mariner 2, the first planetary probe.
◆		Bell Labs shines a laser beam to the moon.

- Rachel Carson publishes *Silent Spring*, a book describing the environmental impact of pesticides. It inspires people to consider the negative impacts of technology and marks the beginning of the modern environmental movement.
- Philips introduces the audiocassette.
- The LED (light-emitting diode) is introduced.
- Unimation markets the first industrial robots, and General Motors installs them for operation in its assembly line.

1963

Feb 1   The U.S. creates the Communications Satellite Corporation (Comsat) as a private company to work with other nations in establishing a network of communications satellites.

May 7   Telstar 2 is launched.

June 19   The U.S.S.R. launches Vostok 2, and Valentine Tereshkova becomes the first woman in space.

Aug 30   The U.S. and U.S.S.R. establish a hot line, or direct telephone link, between the White House and the Kremlin.

Nov 27   The U.S. launches the Interplanetary Monitoring Platform (IMP), the first satellite to use integrated circuits.

- Edwin Land introduces the Polaroid self-developing color camera.
- U.S. Congress passes the nation's first Clean Air Act.
- The first transatlantic cable between the U.S. and Europe is completed, linking Tuckerton, N.J. and Cornwall, England.

1964

Feb 14   Zenith introduces a hearing aid which is the first commercial device using an integrated circuit.

Mar 19   John Kemeny and Thomas Kurtz develop BASIC, a computer language for beginners.

Apr 7   IBM introduces the System/360 family of mainframe computers, which leads to the company's dominance of the industry.

June 18   An underwater telephone cable between the U.S. and Japan begins service.

Aug 19   The U.S and 11 other nations form the International Satellite Organization (Intelsat).

Oct 12   The Soviet Voskhod 1 becomes the first spacecraft to carry multiple passengers.

- Arthur J. Minasy invents the anti-shoplifting tag.
- Paul Baran suggests the concept of a decentralized computer network, which forms the basis of what eventually evolves into the Internet.

1965

Mar 18   The U.S.S.R. launches Voskhod 2, and Aleksei Leonov becomes the first person to complete a spacewalk.

Apr	6	Intelsat launches Early Bird, also called Intelsat 1. It is the first commercial communications satellite in geosynchronous orbit.
June	3	The U.S. launches Gemini 4, and Edward White performs the first American spacewalk while an international television audience watches the event.
Aug	21	The American Gemini 5 space mission is the first to use fuel cells to generate electricity.
◆		U.S. Congress passes the Motor Vehicle Air Pollution Control Act.

1966

Feb	3	The Soviet Luna 9 performs the first soft landing on the moon.
Mar	16	The American Gemini 8 performs the first space docking with another vehicle.
◆		Charles Kao and George Hockham publish a paper claiming fiber optic cables to be an effective medium for the transmission of light carrying information.

1967

Jan	27	An accident during a training exercise on the ground kills three American astronauts. They become the first casualties of the space program.
Mar	1	Direct dial telephone service begins from New York to Paris and London.
Apr	24	Soviet cosmonaut Vladimir Komarov becomes the first person to die during a space mission after the parachute of the Soyuz 1 craft malfunctions during his descent to Earth.
◆		U.S. Congress passes the Air Quality Act.

1968

Dec	21	The U.S. launches Apollo 8 and puts the first humans into lunar orbit. It is also the first time the Saturn 5 rocket is used for a space mission.
Dec	31	The Soviet Tupolev TU-144 becomes the first supersonic transport (SST) airliner to fly.
◆		James Powell and Gordon Danby patent their idea for a superconducting magnetically levitated (maglev) train.
◆		Douglas Engelbart invents the computer mouse.

1969

Mar	2	The Concorde SST, developed by Great Britain and France, makes its first flight. After going into service in 1973, the Concorde proves to be a commercial failure because few customers could afford to fly it, and the noise from its sonic boom creates negative public opinion for the plane.
July	16	The U.S. launches Apollo 11 to the moon.
July	20	The Apollo 11 astronauts become the first humans on the moon.
Dec	19	The U.S. Defense Department sets up ARPANET, a decentralized computer network designed to survive a nuclear attack. ARPANET is the earliest manifestation of the Internet.

◆   Xerox establishes the Palo Alto Research Center (PARC), which develops many concepts used in modern microcomputers.

1970-1979

1970

Jan 21   The Boeing 747 becomes the first jumbo jet to go into service for a commercial airline.

Apr 11   The U.S. launches Apollo 13 to the moon, but an explosion caused by a ruptured oxygen tank forces the crew to prematurely return to Earth.

Sep 19   Robert Maurer, Donald Keck, and Peter Schulz of Corning Glass Works develop an optical fiber suitable for communications purposes.

Dec 15   The Soviet Venera 7 space probe arrives on Venus and performs the first soft-landing on a planet other than Earth.

◆   IBM introduces the floppy disk for storing computer data.

◆   Kenneth Thompson and Dennis Ritchie develop Unix, a computer operating system that becomes the standard for multi-user systems.

1971

Apr 14   Texas Instruments introduces the Pocketronic, the first pocket calculator.

Apr 19   The U.S.S.R. launches Salyut 1, the first space station in orbit.

July 26   The U.S. launches Apollo 15 to the moon where astronauts first use the Lunar Roving Vehicle (LRV), also called the rover.

Nov 15   Intel introduces the 4004 microprocessor. Invented by Marcian "Ted" Hoff, the microprocessor incorporates the major components of a computer on one chip and opens the door to the development of personal computers.

◆   Hoffman–La Roche and Company patents the first commercial LCD (liquid crystal display) system.

◆   Nolan Bushnell creates the video game Pong and founds Atari.

1972

Mar 2   The U.S. launches Pioneer 10, the first space probe to fly to the solar system's outer planets.

May 26   The U.S. and U.S.S.R. sign the Strategic Arms Limitation Treaty (SALT 1), the first agreement limiting the production and deployment of nuclear weapons.

July 23   The U.S. launches ERTS 1 (Earth Resource Technology Satellite), also called Landsat.

◆   The U.S. bans the use of the pesticide DDT.

◆   A study conducted by F. Sherwood Rowland and Mario Jose Molino shows evidence that CFCs damage the earth's ozone layer, a protective shield against the sun's ultraviolet rays.

◆   Hewlett-Packard introduces the HP-35, the first programmable pocket calculator.

1973

Mar	6	The U.S. launches the deep-space probe Pioneer 11.
May	14	The U.S. launches the space station Skylab into orbit.
Oct	19	Middle East oil-producing nations ban shipment of petroleum to the U.S.

1974

June 25	Texas Instruments patents the hand-held electronic calculator, developed by Jack Kilby in 1967.
◆	Electronic scanners using lasers to read bar codes on products are introduced in U.S. supermarkets.
◆	Philips introduces the home video-cassette recorder (VCR), but the N1500 is unsuccessful because the half-inch tapes it uses only run for one hour.

1975

Jan 19	Edward Roberts of MITS introduces the Altair 8800, the first microcomputer.
Feb 19	William (Bill) Gates and Paul Allen develop the first operating system for microcomputers, a version of BASIC for the Altair 8800.
July 15	The U.S. and U.S.S.R. launch their first collaborative manned space mission. Two days later, the American Apollo and Soviet Soyuz spacecraft dock, and the ships' crews conduct experiments together.
◆	Xerox PARC develops the Alto, a computer with many principles later used in the Apple Macintosh. Xerox does not market the Alto.
◆	Michael Shrayer develops the Electric Pencil, the first word processing program for a personal computer.

1976

◆	Genentech, the first genetic engineering company, is founded.
◆	Japan Victor Company (JVC) introduces the VHS format for video tapes, which allows VCRs to gain popularity.

1977

Apr 19	Stephen Wozniak and Steve Jobs introduce the Apple II, the first fully-assembled microcomputer.
May 19	AT&T installs the first commercial fiber optic cables in Chicago.
Aug 20	The U.S. launches the deep-space probe Voyager 2.
Sep 5	The U.S. launches the deep-space probe Voyager 1, which takes a more direct route to the outer planets than Voyager 2.
◆	The Environmental Protection Agency (EPA) blames exposure to toxic chemicals for the high rate of various medical disorders in the Love Canal section of Niagara Falls, New York. More than 1,000 families are relocated over the next three years.
◆	Erno Rubik patents the Rubik's Cube puzzle.

1978

June 11 Texas Instruments introduces the MOS/LSI speech synthesizer chip, which is used in the Speak and Spell talking learning aid for children.

June 19 Apple introduces the floppy disk drive for personal computers.

July 25 Louise Joy Brown, the first test-tube baby, is born. The technique of conceiving babies outside the human body is developed by Robert Edwards and Patrick Steptoe.

1979

Mar 28 An accident at the Three Mile Island nuclear power station forces the evacuation of 144,000 people in Pennsylvania.

Dec 19 Daniel Bricklin and Robert Frankson introduce VisiCalc, the first spreadsheet software for personal computers.

◆ Catalytic converters are introduced to reduce pollution caused by automobile exhaust.

◆ Philips and Sony introduce the videodisk.

1980-1989

1981

Apr 12 The U.S. launches the space shuttle Columbia, the first reusable space vehicle.

July 7 The Solar Challenger, the first solar-powered airplane, flies over the English Channel.

Aug 12 IBM introduces the PC, its first personal computer. Its operating system is MS-DOS, developed by William (Bill) Gates and Paul Allen of Microsoft Corporation.

◆ Adam Osborne introduces the Osborne I, the first portable computer. It has a built-in disk drive, monitor, and keyboard.

1982

Oct Philips and Sony introduce the Compact Disc (CD).

◆ Columbia Data Products introduces the first personal computer compatible with the IBM PC. Other such machines, called clones, quickly saturate the market.

1983

Jan 19 Apple introduces the Lisa personal computer, which utilizes a graphical user interface (GUI) and mouse-operated commands. It is too expensive, however, to succeed commercially.

Feb 19 The IBM PC XT is the first personal computer with a built-in hard disk drive for long-term memory storage.

June 13 Pioneer 10 becomes the first spacecraft to leave the solar system.

June 18 Space shuttle Challenger astronaut Sally Ride becomes the first American woman in space.

Oct 19   Ameritech Mobile Communications initiates the first commercial cellular portable telephone service in the U.S.

◆   A group of scientists introduce the concept of nuclear winter, a condition caused by a large-scale exchange of nuclear weapons which would raise enough dust and smoke to prevent sunlight from reaching the earth.

1984

Jan 23   Apple introduces the Macintosh personal computer, an affordable and user-friendly machine that becomes a commercial success and revolutionizes the industry.

Feb 7   American astronaut Bruce McCandless performs the first untethered space walk using a manned maneuvering unit (MMU).

June 4   Scientists at the University of California clone the DNA of an extinct species of horse.

Nov 19   Philips and Sony introduce the CD-ROM for storage of large amounts of computer data.

Dec 3   Toxic gas leaking from a pesticide plant in Bhopal, India kills thousands of people and leaves thousands more with various injuries and afflictions.

◆   IBM introduces the desktop laser printer.

1985

Sep 1   Robert Ballard uses a remote-controlled robot with a video camera to discover the remains of the Titanic.

Nov 20   Microsoft introduces Windows, a graphical operating system similar to the one used by the Macintosh, for IBM compatible microcomputers.

◆   Paul Brainard develops PageMaker, the first desktop publishing software for personal computers.

1986

Jan 19   K. Alex Müller and J. George Bednorz discover that certain ceramics have superconductive properties at much higher temperatures than metals.

Jan 28   The American space shuttle Challenger explodes 73 seconds after lift-off, killing all seven astronauts on-board.

Feb 19   Great Britain and France sign the Channel Tunnel Treaty.

Feb 20   The U.S.S.R. launches the Mir space station into orbit.

Apr 26   An explosion at the Chernobyl nuclear power plant in the U.S.S.R. sends radioactive clouds across Europe.

1987

Jan 28   Paul Ching-Wu Chu and Maw-Kuen Wu create a ceramic that superconducts the unprecedented temperature of 93 Kelvin.

Oct 19   Computerized trading on Wall Street causes the greatest single-day loss in the history of the New York Stock Exchange.

1988

- The first trans-Atlantic fiber optic cable is installed. It is capable of transmitting more than 37,000 telephone calls.
- The U.S. Air Force unveils the B-2 stealth bomber, an airplane designed to be undetectable by radar.
- The first transatlantic fiber optic telephone cable is completed between the U.S. and Europe.

1989

Mar 23   B. Stanley Pons and Martin Fleischmann announce that they have succeeded in producing a nuclear fusion reaction at room temperature, a process called cold fusion, but other scientists cannot duplicate or confirm the results.

Mar 24   The oil tanker Exxon Valdez ruptures its hull in the waters of Alaska and causes the worst oil spill in U.S. history.

May 2   Eighty nations sign a United Nations agreement to phase out CFC production by the year 2000.

Dec 19   The U.S. Air Force uses the F-117A stealth fighter in combat for the first time.

- Tim Berners-Lee invents the World Wide Web (WWW) as part of the Internet.
- The first transpacific fiber-optic telephone cable between the continental U.S., Hawaii, and Japan is completed.

1990-1999

1990

Jan 29   Alan Huang and colleagues at Bell Labs demonstrate the first optical computer processor.

Feb   The American Voyager space probe transmits the first photograph of the solar system to Earth.

Apr 25   The U.S. launches the space shuttle Discovery which deploys the Hubble Space Telescope (HST) into orbit, but the telescope is soon discovered to have a flawed mirror that causes images to be blurred.

- Ballard Power Systems builds the first zero-emissions bus, which is powered by fuel cells.

1991

- General Instrument Corporation develops the first working digital high-definition television (HDTV).

1992

Jan 6   AT&T announces its plans to mass market a videophone that transmits video as well as audio signals through standard telephone lines.

May   22   The first commercial fuel cell generator in the U.S. is installed at the headquarters of the South Coast Air Quality Management District in California.

May   The World Wide Web is released for public use.

◆   Intel releases the flash memory chip, which stores memory like a hard drive but without moving parts.

1993

Jan   12   Vincent Huering and Harry Jordan unveil the first fully-optical computer, which uses light traveling through optical fibers to store and process data.

Feb   A group of students led by Marc Andreesen release Mosaic, a computer program that allows easy navigation of the World Wide Web.

Dec   2   The U.S. launches the space shuttle Endeavor, and its crew repairs the defective Hubble Space Telescope in orbit.

1994

Feb   3   The space shuttle Discovery deploys the Wake Shield Facility (WSF) to produce pure crystals of the semiconductor gallium arsenide in the vacuum of space.

May   6   Queen Elizabeth II of England and French President Francois Mitterrand become the first passengers to ride the Eurostar train through the newly-completed Channel Tunnel, also called the Chunnel.

Oct   14   Netscape releases its first version of Navigator, a World Wide Web browser.

1995

Aug   Microsoft releases Explorer, its first World Wide Web browser.

1996

Jan   26   The Federal Communications Commission (FCC) announces its technical standards for digital high-definition television (HDTV).

May   14   Daimler-Benz unveils NECAR II, a fuel cell-powered minivan prototype.

1997

Feb   22   Ian Wilmut announces his success in genetically cloning an adult sheep.

Feb   Pioneer releases the first DVD (digital video disk) player. A DVD is the same size as a CD, but its greater memory allows it to store an entire movie on one disk. DVDs are also expected to be used for audio and computer data.

Mar   1   Don Wolf and a team of researchers announce the successful genetic cloning of two adult monkeys.

May   11   World chess champion Garry Kasparov was defeated by IBM Deep Blue computer after six games in which Kasparov won the first game and came to draw in the other three.

TECHNOLOGY

chapter 1

1900-1909

Conquest of the Air:
Aviation and Radio

World's first motion picture camera, Edison's 1889 strip kinetograph

Technology didn't take long to make its mark on the 20th century. Three major milestones of the century's technology have their roots in its first decade: aviation, mass communication, and the production of synthetic materials. The invention of the airplane, radio, and plastic had humble beginnings, but spawned massive worldwide industries dedicated to improving and marketing them.

The people who developed these technologies possessed the vision and ingenuity to take existing concepts and successfully mold them into new breakthroughs. These were among the last of the independent inventors Eventually, corporations, governments, and research foundations, with resources far beyond the means of individuals, began to dominate the pursuit of technological innovation. In this light, it is remarkable that some of the century's most noteworthy and far-reaching inventions were created by individuals with such limited material

Wilbur Wright flies biplane glider, 1902

resources. These inventors, however, proved that by fully utilizing their most important resource — their imagination — the sky was indeed the limit.

The political world, however, did not enter the century with such immediate change. As in previous centuries, European imperialism still dominated the planet. The British Empire, at its peak, was the most expansive dominion, spanning about one-fifth of the planet's land surface and governing one-quarter of its population. European-based empires had territories all over the world, and each was hungry for more power.

As tensions increased, nations began to create alliances. The Triple Alliance of Germany, Austria-Hungary, and Italy was formed in 1887. France and Russia followed with their own agreement in 1890. Driven by its desire for greater world power, Germany passed the second Navy Law in 1900 with the objective of doubling the size of its navy within 20 years. Britain and France had been competing colonial powers in the 19th century, but, fearing the growth of German military strength, the two nations settled their diplomatic differences in 1904 with the Entente Cordiale. Russia's 1907 agreement with Britain completed the anti-German coalition called the Triple Entente. With the opposing alliances in place, an arms race followed; the stage was being set for a world war.

The United States, just coming into its own as a world power after 1898's Spanish-American War, refused to get involved in these European matters. The new century in America brought along with it a presidential assassination on September 6, 1901, when self-proclaimed anarchist Leon Czolgosz shot President William McKinley. McKinley died on September 14, leaving the presidency to a 43-year-old Theodore Roosevelt.

Soon after taking the helm, Roosevelt attempted to negotiate an agreement with Colombia to build and control a canal through Panama, which was then part of Colombia. When these negotiations failed, Roosevelt sent the Panamanian rebels military support and helped them secede from Colombia. The newly formed Republic of Panama declared its independence in 1903 and promptly granted the United States the right to proceed with its canal-building plans under the Hay-Bunau-Varilla Treaty. Construction of the mammoth project began in 1904 and lasted 10 years.

As this engineering marvel that created a new avenue for an old vehicle was being built, an entirely new type of vehicle was being introduced to a world grounded in skepticism.

Orville and Wilbur Wright

Learning to Fly

Since the earliest times, the ability to fly has been one of humankind's loftiest dreams. It is reflected in mythologies from all over the world and is often considered a power reserved for supernatural beings or heroes. One of the first people to approach the possibility of flight was Italian Renaissance artist and scientist Leonardo da Vinci, whose notebooks from the early 16th century contain designs for various flying machines. Two french papermakers, the brothers Joseph-Michel and Jacques-Etienne de Montgolfier, were the first to solve the puzzle of manned flight when they invented the hot-air balloon in 1783. Although lighter-than-air craft such as hot-air balloons allowed people to fly, they were not self-powered and difficult to control.

In the early 19th century, Englishman George Cayley built a series of full-scale model gliders that were sent on numerous unpiloted flights. Although unconfirmed, legend has it that Cayley's coachman became the first person to fly in a heavier-than-air craft.

Otto Lilienthal, a German engineer, continued where Cayley left off by constructing and flying in his own gliders. Lilienthal's flying machines were primitive versions of today's hang gliders. Between 1891 and 1896 he completed almost 2,000 successful flights with 18 different glider designs. He attempted to achieve stability and balance by shifting the weight of his body, but this approach proved disastrous when Lilienthal plunged to his death during one of his flights in 1896.

Like balloons, gliders are not self-powered, and flights in these machines are not considered free flight. To achieve free flight, an aircraft must take off and remain airborne by its own power and

1903 Wright Brothers flyer

The possibility of sustained free flight now seemed unlikely. This mood was reflected in a *New York Times* story following Langley's last crash: "We hope that Prof. Langley will not put his substantial greatness as a scientist in further peril by continuing to waste his time, and the money involved, in further airship experiments."

Unlike the renowned Langley, the brothers **Orville** and **Wilbur Wright** were not scientists. They were bicycle makers from Dayton, Ohio, who had also been in the printing business. Their entrepreneurial success gave them the time and resources to tackle the problems of free flight, and in 1899 they began their historic mission.

control on an upward or level path, and land on ground as high as that from which it took off. At the turn of the century, inventors still struggled to solve the problem of free flight.

Dr. **Samuel P. Langley**, secretary of the Smithsonian Institution, took the next major step by incorporating a power source into an aircraft. He made history in 1896 when two of his powered models flew over Washington, D.C.'s, Potomac River. Called "aerodromes," these machines were unmanned, but the successful flights secured government funding for Langley to develop a self-propelled, piloted aircraft. On October 7, 1903, after years of dedicated work, Langley put his aerodrome to the test. Piloted by Charles Manly, it took off over the Potomac and promptly plummeted into the river. In a second attempt on December 8, again with Manly at the controls, the machine fell tail first into the icy water and was badly damaged. With this failed attempt, Langley's pursuit of powered flight came to an abrupt end.

Based on the work of their predecessors, the Wright brothers knew that stability, control, and a light-enough power source were crucial to achieving free flight. Ironically, their lack of formal training may have helped them because they were not limited by any preconceptions. As Wilbur pointed out, they had to find out for themselves. "Those who tried to study the science of aerodynamics knew not what to believe," he said. "Things which seemed reasonable were very often found to be untrue, and things

"A bird is an instrument working according to mathematical law...which it is within the capacity of man to reproduce."

Leonardo da Vinci

which seemed unreasonable were sometimes true. Under this condition of affairs, students were accustomed to pay little attention to things that they had not personally tested."

And so the Wright brothers began their systematic approach to solving the age-old riddle of free flight. Paying close attention to the true experts, they observed birds and learned to imitate various wing motions with their arms.

One of the most substantial obstacles for early potential aviators was the problem of making an aircraft sufficiently stable. The Wright brothers, however, intentionally created an unstable airplane making it more sensitive to the pilot's controls. They wanted to fly the plane, rather than letting the plane fly them.

They also needed to solve the problem of control in all three axes of movement: up and down, forward and back, and side to side. Orville and Wilbur devised a system of controlling an airplane known as **"wing-warping"**, in which wires linked the tip of each wing to sticks held by the pilot. The aviator would control the plane by pulling or pushing the sticks, causing the tips of the wings to meet the air at the optimum angles.

The Wrights tested this design with model gliders and then with a full-scale glider at **Kitty Hawk**, a small, isolated fishing village on the coast of North Carolina in the Kill Devil Hills area. The treeless sand dunes and ideal wind conditions provided a perfect testing ground for the Wright brothers' airplanes.

After the first glider test flights, the brothers returned to Dayton, and in 1901 they built

a wind tunnel, a chamber through which air is blown. They used the wind tunnel to study the aerodynamic qualities of more than 200 different types of wings.

During September and October 1902, Orville and Wilbur made more than 700 successful flights at Kitty Hawk with a full-scale, unmanned glider, and in the process they made an important discovery. Until then, their designs had relied on a fixed vertical plane for the tail. By replacing it with a movable flap and linking it to the wing-warping system, they dramatically increased the level of control and stability.

The Wright brothers felt they had come up with a good aeronautical design, and they patented the wing-warping and adjustable tailplane system. Back in Dayton, they began building the **Flyer**, a wooden biplane consisting of two parallel canvas-covered wings spanning 40 feet.

A power source was now the missing link to a free-flying aircraft. Despite recent improvements to the internal combustion engine, the brothers felt they needed a lighter motor if their plane was going to lift off the ground. With the help of their mechanic,

Wright Flyer engine

Charles Taylor, they designed and built from scratch a four-cylinder, 12-horse-power, water-cooled gasoline engine suitable for their purposes. They then built two eight-foot propellers and installed them on the rear of the wings to prevent any turbulence. Next they attached each propeller to the engine with bicycle chains. The engine would spin the propellers in opposite directions to prevent the airplane from tipping to one side.

> **"I confess that in 1901, I said to my brother Orville that man would not fly for fifty years."**
>
> Wilbur Wright, 1908

Orville and Wilbur shipped the Flyer to Kitty Hawk in September 1903, and assembled it there. Strong winds and bitter cold, however, forced the brothers to delay testing their new flying machine until December 14. They tossed a coin to determine who would fly it first — Wilbur won.

The Flyer had no wheels. It took off from a wooden launching rail placed on the sand dunes. Wilbur lay face down in the hip cradle centered on the lower wing. He was unfamiliar with the engine's power and rose too steeply, causing the plane to stall and crash into the sand on his first attempt.

After repairing the damage, the brothers tried again on the cold, gray morning of December 17, only nine days after Professor Langley's second and final failed attempt. It was Orville's turn to fly, and at 10:35 a.m. Wilbur released the restraining cable. The Flyer moved forward slowly into the 27-mile-an-hour wind as Wilbur ran along its right side, holding the wing to help stabilize it.

Nearing the end of the runway, the plane rose into the air, climbing about 10 feet above the dunes. After remaining airborne for 12 seconds, Orville made a rough landing into the sand.

Orville had covered 120 feet at a ground speed of 10 miles an hour. It was humankind's first controlled, powered flight, and a dream come true: He had flown!

John T. Daniels was one of five local spectators to witness the historic event. Before the flight, he and his companions thought the two aviators were crazy, but they soon changed their minds.

"I like to think about that first airplane the way it tailed off in the air at Kill Devil Hills that morning, as pretty as any bird you ever laid your eyes on," Daniels later said. "I don't think I ever saw a prettier sight in my life."

After Orville's successful first flight, Wilbur tried again and flew 175 feet. They each made two flights that day, increasing the distance covered and the flight time with every attempt. Wilbur's final flight lasted 59 seconds, covered 852 feet, and reached speeds of up to 30 miles an hour.

As the two victorious brothers discussed the morning's success, a strong gust of wind blew the plane over and damaged it. They packed up their belongings and went home just in time for Christmas.

They notified the press of their success, but most publications ignored them, thinking it was a hoax like so many other claims had been. The only newspaper to seriously cover the story was the *Norfolk Virginian-Pilot*.

"The problem of aerial navigation without the use of a balloon has been solved at last," the December 18 edition stated.

In May 1904 the brothers invited reporters to witness for themselves the Flyer in action, but prohibited them from taking any photographs because the design was not yet patented. Fifty reporters arrived at the exhibition in Dayton, but poor wind conditions and engine failures prevented a successful flight.

The Wright brothers had conquered the air, but they didn't conquer their doubters until 1908, when, much to the surprise of a skeptical world, Orville and Wilbur held a series of successful public demonstrations in the United States and France. During one of these trials in 1908, at Fort Myer, Virginia, Orville encountered mechanical problems and crashed, killing his passenger, Lieutenant T.E. Selfridge. This was one of the earliest fatal accidents involving free-flying aircraft. Despite the tragedy, the U.S. and France signed military contracts with the Wright brothers the same year.

The United States bought its first warplane in 1909. It was a Wright biplane with a 36-foot wingspan, a top speed of 44 miles an hour, and a 75-mile range.

The world was beginning to recognize the significance of powered flight, but it took another momentous flight the following year to cement its future. In the early morning of July 25, 1909, **Louis Blériot** lifted off from France's Normandy coast in a small monoplane of his own design called the **No. XI**. The plane utilized a wing-warping system like the one used by the Wright brothers. Thirty-seven minutes later, he had flown 23.5 miles across the English Channel and landed near Dover Castle in England.

Blériot had shown the British and the world that the English Channel was no longer a barrier against invasion. As many observers pointed out, Britain was "no longer an island." David Lloyd George, British chancellor of the exchequer and future prime minister, soon declared, "Flying machines are no longer toys and dreams; they are an established fact."

Look, Ma, No Wires

Inventors during the first decade of the century were also engaging in a different kind of conquest of the air: the use of radio waves for communication.

The invention of radio was based largely on previous work. Radio waves had been discovered in the 19th century

Guglielmo Marconi

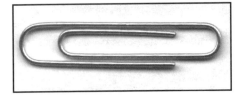

PAPER CLIP:

The turn of the century ushered in the age of the paper clip. The seemingly simple idea was patented in 1900 by Norwegian Johann Vaaler. The paper clip solved the age-old problem of keeping papers bound together. Previous fastening devices over the centuries included pins, which made holes, and unreliable spring-operated clips. During the German occupation of Norway in World War II, Norwegians are said to have worn paper clips on their jacket lapels as symbols of their patriotism and unity despite a Nazi law forbidding such a display. The paper clip's purpose of "binding together" applied not only to paper, but to people.

as a way to transmit electrical signals without wires. In 1888, **Heinrich Hertz** was the first person to send and receive such signals, which he called Hertzian waves. He and other scientists, however, could not find a practical use for transmitting signals without wires.

Like the Wright brothers, **Guglielmo Marconi** was not a scientist, but he did have a technical background and was familiar with electromagnetic theory, which relates to the transmission of energy in the form of waves. In 1894, the year Hertz died, Marconi read about Hertzian waves and came up with the idea of using them to send **Morse code**, a telegraph communication system using short- and long-duration electrical signals known as "dots" and "dashes." Marconi was surprised that no one else had thought of it.

"(It) was so simple in logic," he said, "that it seemed difficult for me to believe that no one else had thought of putting it into practice."

At the age of 20, Marconi set up a laboratory in the attic of his father's estate in Italy. He worked incessantly for months, barely stopping to eat, until one day he called his mother in to show her something. He tapped a telegraph key, and a bell rang on the other side of the attic. There were no connecting wires.

This was a great accomplishment, but there was much more work for Marconi to do. Soon he improved the coherer, a device used for detecting radio waves. He also was the first to use antennas for reception instead of the two lengths of wire, or dipole, used by Hertz. But Marconi still struggled to find a way to send radio waves farther than his own attic. Hertz had used waves that measured only four of five meters in length. Marconi decided to use waves that were hundreds and even thousands of meters, and by 1895 he was sending Morse code 1.5 miles.

After a demonstration of his discoveries failed to impress the Italian government, Marconi moved to England in 1896. In addition to his technical skills, he also had good business sense, and realized that he needed to find the right market for his invention. He decided to target the shipping industry, because it was a large market that telegraph and cable communication could not serve. At the time, Britain was the world's most dominant seafaring nation; more than half of the world's ships were registered there. It was the ideal place for Marconi to set up his business in "wireless telegraphy."

He founded the Marconi Company and received his first patent in 1897. By 1899 he was transmitting radio waves across the English Channel. Scientists acknowledged his success, but most believed that radio waves traveled in a straight line like light and therefore could only reach as far as the visible horizon, which is about 200 miles.

Once again Marconi was a step ahead of his more educated contemporaries. On December 12, 1901, he transmitted three dots — Morse code for the letter "S" — from England to a receiving station in Newfoundland, Canada. He had sent radio waves over 2,137 miles despite the curvature of the earth, an obstacle equivalent to a 250-mile-high mountain of water.

"I now felt for the first time," Marconi said, "absolutely certain that the day would come when mankind would be able to send messages without wires not only across the Atlantic, but between the farthermost ends of the Earth."

Marconi proved his critics wrong and changed the course of communication technology forever, but he couldn't explain how the signals could be transmitted beyond the earth's curvature. The answer would come the following year when British-American **Arthur Kennelly** and Englishman **Oliver Heaviside** postulated the existence of a reflective layer in the atmosphere, which was later to be called the ionosphere. They theorized that radio waves "bounce" off the ionosphere, preventing them from traveling straight into outer space. Amazingly, the two men, working independently on different continents, generated the same theory almost simultaneously.

Lee de Forest

Meanwhile, Marconi continued to improve his invention. By 1904 his radio system was transmitting regular news bulletins to ships in the Atlantic. He won the Nobel Prize for physics in 1909. Marconi's death on July 20, 1937, was commemorated the following day by radio operators around the world who honored his memory by shutting down their transmitters for two minutes.

Marconi is often called "the father of radio," but others were instrumental in its further development. **Reginald A. Fessenden** took Marconi's ideas to a new dimension. Marconi had the foresight to transmit Morse code using radio waves, but the idea of using these waves to transmit voices and music belongs to Fessenden.

Unlike Marconi, Fessenden was well educated in the sciences. Born in Quebec, Canada, he had been inventor **Thomas Edison's** chief chemist at the Edison Machine Works in New Jersey, as well as chief electrician for Edison's rival, Westinghouse Electric Corporation in Massachusetts. He was also a professor of engineering at Purdue University and Western University of Pennsylvania (now the University of Pittsburgh).

Fessenden patented a high-frequency alternator in 1901 that produced a continuous radio wave, an improvement over Marconi's intermittent, spark-generated pulse for Morse code transmission.

For better reception over long distances, Fessenden limited the signal to one frequency. He also used a microphone, like one used in a telephone, to convert sound waves into electric signals. He was the first to use amplitude modulation (**AM**), which matches the amplitude, or height, of a radio wave with the amplitude of the electric signal. After being transmitted by an antenna, the receiver decoded and converted the AM radio waves back into their original sounds.

On Christmas Eve, 1906, with a large generator in Massachusetts that took three years to build, Fessenden transmitted the world's first audio broadcast. Wireless operators on ships in the Atlantic listening for Morse code suddenly heard a man speaking through their headphones, followed by violin music and, finally, a recording of "O Holy Night." Later that year Fessenden transmitted his signals to Scotland and established the first wireless trans-Atlantic voice communication.

One of America's most prolific inventors, Fessenden died in 1932 with over 500 patents in his name.

Another radio innovator, Englishman **John A. Fleming**, made an important discovery in 1904 that greatly improved radio reception. Based on a mysterious experiment performed by Thomas Edison in 1884, Fleming invented the vacuum tube, or diode. Also called the thermionic valve, it used heat to control the flow of electricity and was a very efficient radio-wave detector. American **Lee De Forest** went a step farther in 1906 by adding a third element and creating a triode vacuum tube, or audion.

1906 Audion vacuum tube

The result was a more sensitive detector with improved amplification of weak signals. Vacuum tubes became essential components in radios as well as virtually all other electronic equipment until transistors eventually replaced them in the second half of the century.

The Plastic Men

With the recent birth of radio, humans took another giant technological step by inventing synthetic plastic. The man responsible for this creation was **Leo Hendrik Baekeland**, a Belgian immigrant. Inspired by Benjamin Franklin's autobiography, he came to the United States in 1889 with dreams of becoming rich. Baekeland quickly realized his dream in 1891 when he improved the photographic paper Velox, making it possible to develop photographs cheaply using artificial light. He sold the patent to **George Eastman**, president of Kodak, for $750,000.

Baekeland's early commercial success did not dull his inquisitive nature. His next challenge was to develop an artificial shellac, a protective coating painted onto wood surfaces. At the time, shellac was made from the wings of Southeast Asian insects and was very expensive. He knew that an inexpensive synthetic substitute would be very profitable. His idea was based on a previous discovery by German chemist **Adolf von Baeyer**, who created a synthetic resin as a byproduct of one of his experiments. It was a hard, black, sticky substance that was seemingly useless, but Baekeland thought that if he could find a way to break the resin down into a liquid, it would make a tough and weatherproof shellac.

Although Baekeland never succeeded in creating a synthetic shellac, he came to realize that the hardened form of von

Leo Baekeland

Baeyer's resin could itself be very valuable. By 1907 he had perfected a process that transformed the substance into the world's first fully synthetic plastic. He called it Bakelite, after himself. By mixing the organic ingredients phenol and formaldehyde in a large iron vessel, called a Bakelizer, he could control the conditions of the chemical reaction and produce a highly versatile material.

Bakelite could be molded and hardened into any shape, it could be dyed any color, and it was resistant to solvents, acids, electricity, heat, and water. Used instead of materials like wood, metal, and ceramics, Bakelite was one of the first artificial substitutes for a natural product. Within a few years the new plastic was used in the manufacture of everything from automobiles to radios

Bakelite Mixer

to molded furniture. Bakelite's commercial success made Baekeland a multimillionaire.

Coincidentally, Baekeland was not alone as a plastics pioneer. **James Swinburne**, a Scottish electrical engineer, made the same discovery at about the same time, but through a different approach. Swinburne was studying the transmission of electricity, and a reliable high-voltage insulator was not available. This problem limited transmission distances. In search of a better insulator, he experimented with the same chemicals as Baekeland and had the same results. When he applied for a patent for his breakthrough, Swinburne found that Baekeland had been awarded an identical patent just the day before.

The unfortunate Swinburne went back to work and eventually came up with a substance called **Damard**. Short for "damn hard," Damard was a tough lacquer for protecting polished metal.

When Baekeland visited England in 1916 to establish a subsidiary, he met with Swinburne and made him chairman of the newly formed Bakelite Limited. Swinburne held the position until he retired at the ripe age of 90. He died one month after his 100th birthday.

Baekeland retired in 1939 to a life of self-imposed seclusion in his Florida mansion, growing increasingly untrusting and withdrawn, and eating his meals from tin cans until his death in 1944.

Modern Conveniences

Aviation, wireless communication, and plastic are all technologies unique to the 20th century. They are very complex and innovative breakthroughs, but other advances, perhaps less awe-inspiring, were made during this period, many of which have become an integral part of daily life.

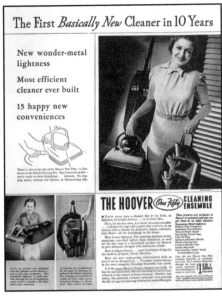

Ad for Hoover vacuum

For instance, the air conditioner was a great idea, but 15 years passed after its invention before anyone thought of using it to make people more comfortable. **Willis H. Carrier** invented the air conditioner in 1902 to improve the conditions for color printing. Its practical application as a climate-control device for humans came into use in 1917 when the owners of the Central Park Theater in Chicago installed air conditioning to attract customers during the hot summer season.

Before Englishman **Herbert Cecil Booth's** invention of the vacuum cleaner in 1902, cleaning a rug required handwashing or repeated whacking with a carpet beater. It was a strenuous — though sometimes therapeutic — process. Booth's first vacuum cleaners were more of a service than a product. They were much larger than today's vacuum cleaners. Booth mounted the huge machines on wagon wheels and parked them in front of the houses to be cleaned. Booth's employees passed hoses as long as 800 feet through the windows to access the rugs. Guests often assembled at vacuum-cleaning parties to watch the transport of dirt through glass-covered segments at various points along the hoses. Smaller portable vacuums, weighing only 92 pounds, became available in the United States in 1905.

New York subway at 116th Street

NEW YORK SUBWAY

In the middle of the 19th century the rapidly growing city of New York was also quickly developing a serious traffic problem. After years of discussion and political obstacles, a plan to install an underground railway was approved in 1894, and construction began in 1900 under the direction of chief engineer William B. Parsons. More than 7,700 men were needed to dig, and built the 21-mile route, primarily with hand tools. It was dangerous work with hundreds of injuries, and at least 44 deaths.

After a day of ceremony and celebration, the Interborough Rapid Transit System (IRT) finally opened on October 27, 1904. More than 100,000 well-dressed New Yorkers flocked to the new subway on its opening day. The IRT was not the world's first subway — the London Underground railroad gained that distinction when it began operation in 1863 — but it was and is still the most extensive system in the world. New York's underground railway succeeded in reducing street traffic and allowed the city's population to disperse into areas farther from downtown.

Maytag's first washing machine

curved dash, which provided a unique element of style. The **Merry Oldsmobile** also was the first model equipped with a speedometer.

Henry Ford would soon take the mass production of automobiles to new heights and revolutionize the industry, but in 1908 Cadillac became the first company to assemble cars using interchangeable parts. That same year, Ford launched production of the famous Model T. Until then, only the rich could afford cars, but the Model T made owning a car possible for the average person. It was the first "people's car."

The technological developments of the 20h century's first decade in the fields of transportation and communication set the tone for decades to come. Because people and information were gaining the ability to traverse greater distances more quickly and more easily, the notion of a shrinking world was beginning to materialize.

The automobile already had been invented, but its development blossomed after the turn of the century. In 1900, the **Packard Model C** became the first car to use a steering wheel. Before this time, cars were controlled by tillers, similar to the steering devices used on boats.

When **Ransom E. Olds** produced the Oldsmobile in 1901, it became America's first mass-produced automobile. By 1904 Americans had bought 12,000 Oldsmobiles with the famous

TECHNOLOGY

chapter 2

1910-1919

Mass Production and Mass Destruction

Edison Storage battery, 1910

The 20th century is often called the century of technology, but a more ominous nickname is at least as appropriate: the century of wars. The concept of the world war is unique to this century. At the time, World War I was somewhat optimistically known as "the war to end all wars." Ironically, Germany's reaction to World War I's aftermath is what led to World War II only two decades later.

World War I, also called the Great War, was largely the result of rapidly escalating tensions between European nations due to rising nationalism, colonial and economic rivalry, and the hunger for greater power. With the intricate Alliance system in place, a major war seemed inevitable; it was only a matter of time before something set it off. The spark came on June 28, 1914, when Serbian nationalist Gavrilo Princip assassinated Archduke Franz Ferdinand, the heir to the Austro-Hungarian throne. Austria-Hungary declared war on Serbia on July 28, and began to shell Belgrade, Serbia's capital, the following day.

The rest of Europe, and eventually much of the world, soon mobilized into combat. On one side were the Central Powers led by Germany, Austria-Hungary, Bulgaria, and the Ottoman (Turkish) Empire. Opposing them were the Allies led by Great Britain, France, Russia, Japan, and Italy.

Both sides dug an extensive system of fortified trenches to maintain their positions. These defensive measures were very effective and prevented either side from making any significant strategic advances. The majority of the war was locked in a bloody stalemate, with two entrenched lines stretching from the English Channel to Switzerland. The Battle of the Somme, for example, cost 420,000 British and 200,000 French lives between July and November 1916, but only gained six miles of land for the Allies.

While the Russian army was suffering heavy casualties on the front, Russia's poverty-stricken population became increasingly discontented with its czarist government. A revolution overthrew Czar Nicholas II in 1917, and, under the communist leadership of Vladimir Lenin, Russia withdrew from the war the same year.

The United States initially remained neutral, but due mainly to Germany's aggressive use of submarines, it joined the Allied Powers in April 1917. America's entry into the war helped tilt the balance and win the war for the Allies. World War I ended with an armistice on November 11, 1918. It was the first time the German army had ever lost a war. The casualties on both sides of the conflict were astronomical; an estimated 10 million died and 20 million were wounded.

WWI German aviator dropping bomb

Parking lot of Ford Model T's

The victorious Allies organized the Paris Peace Conference and signed the Treaty of Versailles, hoping it would prevent future wars. The treaty forced Germany to accept responsibility and guilt for instigating the war, and required it to pay reparations — financial compensation—to the Allies for their losses. It also severely limited Germany's military size and weapons production.

The war had been a testing ground for a vast array of new weapons. Wartime usually inspires great technological advances, and World War I spawned more new military technology than any other war in history. With the notable exception of the atomic bomb, most of the weapons used during World War II were improvements or adaptations of those used first in World War I. The airplane, submarine and tank were major factors in World War II, but all three were first used in battle during World War I. Poison gas was so horrifying that it was banned by the Geneva

Protocol of 1925 and not used by either side in World War II.

But prior to World War I, a more peaceful revolution was taking place, led by American industrialist Henry Ford. Before he started selling cars, most people relied on horses, trains, and their own legs for transportation. All this changed after Ford began producing the legendary Model T.

More Cars for More People

Henry Ford didn't invent the automobile. Nor did he invent mass production or the assembly line. Ford is famous because he took these existing concepts and incorporated them into an efficient, large-scale system of manufacturing inexpensive, reliable cars.

"I am going to democratize the automobile," Ford said, "and when I'm through, everybody will be able to afford one and about everybody will have one."

AUTOMOBILE SELF-STARTER

Before Charles Kettering of Dayton Engineering Laboratories Company (Delco) invented the self-starter in 1911, the only way to start a car was by turning a hand crank at the front of the vehicle. Hand cranking was a strenuous procedure that also had the potential of causing a broken arm if the engine's compression forced the handle back. Female drivers were rare in the days of the crankshaft, because few women were physically strong enough to operate the mechanism. The women who did drive were often dependent on men for assistance with starting the car. The self-starter allowed women to gain a certain degree of independence by being able to drive without a man's help.

As the son of a farming family in Michigan, he could relate to the common people, and after he introduced the **Model T** in 1908 the commoners made Ford America's first billionaire.

Ford's philosophy was to cut costs by standardizing the manufacture of his product. With greater efficiency, prices would decrease, which would expand the market and increase profits in a continuous cycle. In 1899 Ford formed the **Detroit Automobile Company**, which was later renamed the Henry Ford Company. Ford attempted to implement these mass-production principles, but his financial backers didn't share his optimism. Ford left, and his old company became the Cadillac Automobile Company. To achieve his goals, he founded the Ford Motor Company in 1903. The first Model T hit the market in 1908, and, for efficiency's sake, it was the only model Ford produced during the next two decades.

Ford used two main assembly lines in the Model T's production — one for the chassis and engine and another for the body. At the end, the two components were bolted together, and the car was ready to go.

Nicknamed the **"Tin Lizzie"**, the tough, reliable Model T sold for $850 in 1908, making it affordable in rural and small-town markets. According to one of many old jokes, a gentleman asked to be buried in his Model T because "the darned thing pulled me out of every hole I ever got into, and it ought to pull me out of that one."

"The jokes about my car sure helped to popularize it," Ford once said. "I hope they never end."

1912 Cadillac featuring self-starting engine

In 1908 the rural and small-town market consisted of about half of America's population and was largely untapped by the automobile industry. The Tin Lizzie proved to be very useful to farmers and, when needed, was very easy to repair; it was the perfect car for this vast pool of potential buyers.

> **"Everything in life is somewhere else, and you get there in a car."**
>
> E.B. White, *One Man's Meat*

Ford's innovative mass-production techniques turned his business into an unparalleled success. Rather than having workers bring the components to the work station, Ford's system called for these parts to be brought to the worker.

Ford further increased efficiency in 1913 with the introduction of the moving assembly line, probably his single greatest contribution to modern manufacturing. Conveyor belts would move the automobiles to workers at various stages of production, while separate conveyor belts brought them the necessary interchangeable parts. The operation required detailed planning in order to be perfectly synchronized. Under this system, workers needed very little skill to do their repetitive and tedious jobs.

Before Ford adopted the moving assembly line, a Model T took about 12.5 hours to build. After 1913 it took just over an hour and a half; the Dearborn, Michigan, plant was producing 1,000 cars each day, and the price dropped to $500.

That same year, Ford began limiting his cars to one color: black. Until then, the Model T had also been available in blue, green, red, and gray, but Ford soon discovered that black paint dried the fastest. Since this kept the assembly lines moving at their maximum speed, he discontinued the other colors. The decision prompted Ford to issue his famous statement that the customer could have a Model T in any color he or she wanted, as long as it was black.

(l. to r.) Henry Ford, President Herbert Hoover, and Thomas Edison

The Model T, with its four-cylinder, 20-horsepower engine, was a no-nonsense automobile equipped with only the basic necessities to perform reliably. By 1916 the price was down to $360.

"No car under $2,000 offers more," a Ford advertisement claimed, "and no car over $2,000 offers more except in trimmings."

As the output of cars increased, workers began to complain that assembly-line work was monotonous and dehumanizing. Ford responded by announcing an employee profit-sharing plan that increased salaries to $5 a day, more than doubling their previous wages. His motivation behind this move was not merely to appease his workers; employees earning higher wages meant more consumers who could afford to buy Ford automobiles.

Ford also wanted profits to be used for the company's expansion. His stockholders opposed him, preferring instead to keep their short-term financial gains. Determined to run his business his way, Ford bought them out in 1919.

In retrospect, it appears he knew what he was doing. By 1925 half of the cars in the world were Model Ts. Ford built the Tin Lizzie for 19 years, and the car remained essentially the same during that entire period.

After **Charles Kettering** invented the **electric self-starter** in 1911, Ford incorporated it into the next year's Model T, replacing the hand crank as an easier and safer way of starting a car. This was one of only a few changes made in the Tin Lizzie's long history.

Ford refused to change a design that obviously worked, but his inflexibility eventually backfired. Consumers' tastes began to change. Style and comfort became an important factor in buying a car, and the antiquated Model T just didn't live up to the standards of the day.

In 1927 the last Model T rolled out of the Ford factory. The plant then closed for a year while engineers planned a new design for a new model. It was the end of a long line of more than 15 million nearly identical cars — an unprecedented production run, to be surpassed only by the Volkswagen Beetle in 1972.

As automobiles began to populate the planet, the need for suitable roads increased. White lines were first painted down the center of roads in Redlands, California. In 1914 work began on the first transcontinental road, the Lincoln Highway, stretching from New York City to San Francisco. The first stop signs and electric traffic signals were installed that same year.

The demand for fuel was also rapidly increasing. Gasoline used to power cars requires refining from its raw source, petroleum. In the early days of automobiles, "straight-run" gasoline was used, which was distilled, or vaporized, from crude oil. This process was inefficient, and after Ford's success with the Model T in 1908, oil refineries could not produce enough gasoline to fulfill the demand.

In 1912 William Burton of Standard Oil solved this problem by developing and patenting a refining process called thermal cracking. This improved method used heat and pressure to break down the heavy hydrocarbons in crude oil into the lighter carbons used in gasoline. Burton's employers were initially skeptical of his idea, but by the end of the year 240 Standard plants were operating under the new principles, and the company's profits skyrocketed.

Battle Lines in the Sky

In addition to the popularization of the automobile, World War I was another major reason for the dramatic increase in petroleum demand. Military vehicles including cars, trucks, airplanes, tanks, and ships needed fuel to operate. Many of these vehicles had never been tested in battle before, and along with the proliferation of new weapons, warring nations achieved levels of military strength beyond anything the world had ever witnessed.

Aviation was still in its infancy when the war started, but the new technology was growing up quickly as a number of new innovations were rapidly implemented.

In 1910, Frenchman **Henri Fabre** attached floats to an airplane in place of wheels and thus flew the first seaplane. Two years later, American **Glenn Curtiss** improved the design and made it practical. He demonstrated the seaplane's military potential by landing it near a U.S. Navy ship and using a crane to lift it onto the ship's deck. Although not nearly as famous as the land-based planes, seaplanes were used in World War I for reconnaissance, bombing, and torpedo attacks.

Curtiss also demonstrated the concept of an aircraft carrier when pilot **Eugene Ely** took off from the deck of a ship in a Curtiss plane in 1910. Ely followed up by performing a landing on a ship the following year. Aircraft carriers, however, did not begin to be used in combat until World War II.

In 1911 the Italian army became the first to use airplanes for military purposes

1918 airplane of sound locator

in their war with the Ottoman Turks. The Italians used their aircraft mainly for reconnaissance and observation in Libya. Later that year, an Italian pilot became the first to use an aircraft for ground-attack purposes when he dropped four hand grenades onto the enemy from his airplane.

One of the major structural innovations in aviation came in 1912, with the introduction of the "monocoque" fuselage. The fuselage is the central part of the airplane's length, and, until that time, had been mainly a wooden skeleton held together at intervals by braces and covered with canvas. This skeleton supported the weight of the load being carried. The stronger monocoque fuselage was a single tubular wooden shell rather than a skeleton.

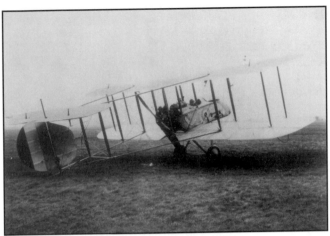

The British Vickers F.B.5

At the outbreak of the war in 1914, the nations involved immediately recognized the strategic importance of air power, and each side attempted to gain the upper hand in the skies. Aircraft were initially used strictly for reconnaissance. Pilots observed and reported enemy locations, movements of supplies, and locations of munitions dumps. These missions proved their significance early in the war. On August 22, 1914, British General Sir John French received reports from reconnaissance pilots that the German army had altered its course en route to Paris. Based on this information, the Allies strengthened their position at the Marne River and repelled the German advance. The defeat was the German army's first major setback of the war, and possibly prevented it from taking Paris at that early stage.

There were two basic types of airplanes. The tractor design had an elongated fuselage with the engine at the front and the pilot behind it. The pusher model had a shorter fuselage with the engine behind the pilot. The tractor's better aerodynamic design meant superior performance; the pusher's advantage was an excellent forward view. Both designs were built as biplanes and monoplanes, although the monoplane had a reputation for being fragile and was much less common. The planes had two seats: one for the pilot and one for an observer.

At first, enemy pilots waved to one another as they flew by, but as the war progressed, these relationships became more adversarial. Pilots and observers began carrying handguns and rifles and fired them at the opposition. This practice proved ineffective and led to the installation of machine guns on aircraft, which led to the birth of aerial combat and the development of fighter planes. To gain the advantage over the opposition these new planes needed to be faster, fly higher at a quicker rate, and be more maneuverable to obtain a tactically superior combat position.

The British **Vickers F.B.5** was the world's first fighter plane. Nicknamed the **Gunbus**, it was a two-seat pusher biplane with a machine gun mounted at the front. The gunner occupied the front seat, which offered the superior view of the field of fire.

Because the Gunbus was a pusher, its performance was inferior, but the problem with mounting machine guns on tractor airplanes was the obstruction of gunfire by the forward propeller. To overcome this problem, French engineer **Raymond Saulnier** installed metal deflectors on the propeller of a plane flown by Roland Garros in 1915. All the pilot had to do now was aim the plane at his target and press the trigger. Garros wreaked havoc on the German lines by firing on them from above, and shot down five German reconnaissance planes in three weeks. His luck ran out on April 10 when he was forced to crash land behind enemy lines and was captured. The perplexed Germans examined his plane and adopted the deflector shields for their propellers, but their machine guns were too powerful for the deflectors and shot the blades off. Determined to gain air superiority, the German high command commissioned aircraft designer **Anthony Fokker** to make the deflectors work with the German guns. Fokker instead came up with an entirely different and better system that synchronized the rotation of the propeller with the firing of the machine gun.

Eddie Rickenbacker

"The obvious thing to do was to make the propeller shoot the gun," Fokker said, "instead of trying to shoot the bullets through the propeller."

In 48 hours he had a working prototype that momentarily interrupted the machine gun's fire when the blades passed in front of the barrel. Fokker installed the device on one of his own airplanes and successfully air-tested it. The German army was pleased, and placed an order with Fokker for his new aircraft. With the introduction of the Fokker **Eindecker** monoplane, the world's first true single-seat fighter was born. Armed with the excellent synchronized 7.92-millimeter Parabellum machine gun, the Eindecker was almost always victorious in battle. It was so superior in the skies over the Western Front that disgruntled Allied pilots referred to their own planes as "Fokker fodder," and the period from autumn 1915 to spring 1916 is remembered as the Fokker Scourge.

The Allies, however, soon responded, and began to challenge the Germans in the air with impressive fighters of their own. The French introduced the

The Red Baron

ZIPPER

▬ ▬ ▬ ▬ ▬ ▬ ▬ ▬ ▬ ▬

Perhaps not be as impressive an engineering feat as the Panama Canal, a device now known as the zipper also uses a series of locks but has had a greater impact on people's daily lives. Whitcomb L. Judson had patented a design for a slide fastener in 1893. Judson's Automatic Hook & Eye Company in New Jersey began marketing it as the "C-curity" fastener in 1904, but it was notorious for popping open and was inefficient to manufacture. After years of dedicated work, he was unable to perfect the mechanism.

Judson's luck changed in 1908, when Gideon Sundback, a former Westinghouse engineer, became fascinated with the concept and began working for him. In 1913 Sundback developed the first practical and successful slide fastener and invented efficient machinery to manufacture it.

Clothing companies initially ignored Sundback's fastener, but in 1918 the U.S. Navy agreed to a contract with Judson's company, now called the Hookless Fastener Company, to supply flying suits using the improved device. Soon other manufacturers began to incorporate the fastener into merchandise such as shoes, gloves, and tobacco pouches in place of buttons, snaps, and buckles. The B.F. Goodrich Company introduced its rubber galoshes with Sundback's fastener in 1923, and called the shoes Zipper Boots. The term "zipper" eventually became the common name for the slide fastener.

Nieuport 11, or Bébé. This highly maneuverable fighter outperformed the Eindecker and had a machine gun mounted on the upper wing that fired over the propeller. Britain's contribution was the de Havilland D.H.2, with which the Royal Flying Corps formed in 1916 its first squadron equipped entirely with single-seat fighters. The Allied forces' new planes suddenly outclassed the previously superior Fokkers and took their turn at ruling the skies.

This back-and-forth shifting of air superiority continued throughout the war as each side introduced increasingly advanced fighters with more powerful engines, better designs, and improved armaments. Some examples are Germany's Albatros, which had the advantage of two guns rather than just one; France's high-performance SPAD XIII, and Britain's Sopwith Camel, which shot down more German planes than any other Allied fighter in the war.

While the heroic exploits of fighter pilots like American Eddie Rickenbacker and German Manfred von Richthofen

A zeppelin ascending

(**the Red Baron**) became famous, aerial bombing was a strategically more important function.

The earliest aerial bombs of the war were not intended to inflict any physical damage; they were a means for the Germans to disperse propaganda. Between August and October 1914, German pilots flying over Paris dropped written messages to instill fear into their enemy.

"The German army is at the gates of Paris," one such message read. "There is nothing for you to do but surrender."

Soon after, pilots began dropping explosives, but their planes did not have bombsights, and hitting the target was largely a matter of luck. These small aircraft were also unable to carry bomb loads large enough to inflict serious damage.

In the war's early stages, the Germans began to use **Zeppelin airships** as their primary bombers. Named after **Count Ferdinand von Zeppelin**, the man who perfected their design, these famous airships, also called **dirigibles**, could carry more payload and fly higher and longer than the airplanes of the period.

Count Zeppelin first flew one of his airships in 1900. The rigid, cigar-shaped, hydrogen-filled airship had an aluminum framework covered with cloth. Although it flew, Zeppelin's first airship had problems, and he perfected the design during the rest of the decade. In 1910 he began the German Airship Transport Company (German acronym **DELAG**), providing transport between German cities. DELAG's five improved Zeppelins carried more than 35,000 passengers safely to their destinations by 1914.

During the war, the Germans began sending Zeppelins on regular bombing raids over England in January 1915. The first such attack over London came in May of that year. These raids caused little physical damage, but the 640-foot-long airships hovering over England in broad daylight were a major intimidating factor and proved to have a significant psychological effect on the British early in the war.

As fighter planes began to evolve into more advanced flying machines and pilots became more experienced, the Zeppelins, filled with highly explosive hydrogen, became more vulnerable to attack. The British defenders scored their first Zeppelin kill in June 1915, when Flight Sub-Lieutenant **Alexander Warneford** flew above a German dirigible and dropped a bomb on it. The Victoria Cross, for valor, was Warneford's reward, but he died 10 days later when his plane crashed.

Germany's heaviest attack, involving 16 Zeppelins carrying 32 tons of bombs, occurred on September 2, 1916. Only four British citizens lost their lives, while the Germans lost 16 crew members and a brand-new airship. The Zeppelins were becoming less effective, and the Germans stopped using them as bombers in October 1917.

By this time both sides of the conflict had begun to use winged bombers, airplanes specifically designed for bombing missions. The British introduced the **D.H.4** bomber in 1917. Considered one of the best aircraft of the war, the D.H.4 was used extensively by both British and American forces for day bombing. For night bombing, the British used the **Handley Page 0/100**.

Discouraged by the Zeppelin's vulnerability, the Germans also turned to bomber planes. Their most famous bombers, the **Gothas**, began taking over for the Zeppelins in 1917. In a series of early raids over England, these aircraft proved substantially more effective by inflicting heavy casualties on the British and eluding their defenses.

With the advent of aerial bombing, the world was faced with an entirely new form of warfare. Gone were the days when civilians could feel safe at home while soldiers faced the enemy at the front line. Civilians were no longer safe; no one was safe from a weapon with wings.

At the beginning of the war, airplanes had an average top speed of 70 miles per hour and a maximum altitude, or ceiling, of 9,000 feet. By 1918, some planes were flying at more than 130 miles per hour and at almost 30,000 feet, the approximate cruising altitude of modern jet airliners.

The advances were rapid indeed, but one of the most important and far-reaching innovations in airplane design during this period occurred too late to be used much in battle. Until the end of the war, all airplanes were wooden and most were biplanes. Professor **Hugo Junkers**, a German engineer, changed the course of aircraft design by building the first successful all-metal airplane. This monoplane was also the first to employ cantilevered wings, which are supported by the body without external bracing.

1916 Boeing utility plane

Junkers patented an aircraft design called a **"flying wing"** in 1910 but never built it. Five years later, undaunted by his government's lack of faith in his proposal, he funded and built the revolutionary **JI** airplane based on these plans.

"I am fully aware that (with untested methods) the likelihood of success is less than along the conventional paths," Junkers had said. "But why should we not tackle problems that may hold tremendous possibilities?"

Junkers originally planned to build his plane with aluminum, but this metal was too scarce during the war years, so he used sheet iron to cover the framework's iron tubing. The **Tin Donkey**, as it was called, made its first flight in December 1915. A battle-ready attack version of the JI flew its first combat mission in 1917, but its performance was not up to par with its contemporaries. An improved version, the Junkers **CL I**, appeared in 1918, and would have helped the Germans' cause had the war not ended late that year.

After peace was restored, aviation was free to be used for civillian purposes. The U.S. Army began operating the first air mail service in 1918. The maiden flight on May 15, with President Woodrow Wilson and thousands of spectators present, had its problems as the aircraft attempted to leave Washington, D.C., with an empty fuel tank. Once refueled, the plane took off successfully for New York, but flew off in the wrong direction. The lost pilot landed in a field in Maryland, and his mail cargo was sent to its destination by train.

Despite this embarrassing inauguration, service improved and the U.S. Post Office took over operations in August. Air mail became well established in the eastern U.S., with 1,208 flights completed in the first year and the opening of

GARRETT A. MORGAN

The African-American inventor of the gas mask, or safety hood, encountered substantial difficulties marketing his device because of widespread racial prejudice. Morgan went on a promotional tour to boost sales of the safety hood and even attempted to disguise his racial identity by posing as "Big Chief Mason," a Canadian Indian, but it did not help.

Unable to profit from the gas mask, Morgan invented another safety device: the first automatic three-way traffic signal with a yellow light to warn drivers to proceed with caution when the light was about to change from green to red. The first electric traffic signals were installed in Cleveland, Ohio, on August 5, 1914, but used buzzers instead of yellow lights. After patenting his traffic signal in 1923, Morgan sold it to General Electric for $40,000 rather than attempting to market it himself.

the New York-Chicago route in May 1919.

While Americans were pioneering air mail delivery, Europeans were concentrating on transporting passengers through the air. The British company **Aircraft Transport and Travel** began passenger service between London and Paris on August 25, 1919. Ten years after Louis Blériot's first crossing of the English Channel, it became almost commonplace.

Just as Blériot's historic flight in 1909 had demonstrated the airplane's significance in narrowing geographic distances, another great aerial crossing came in 1919, this time over the Atlantic.

The British team of Captain **John Alcock** and Lieutenant **Arthur Whitten Brown** departed from Newfoundland, Canada, on June 14 and headed for Ireland in a converted **Vickers Vimy** bomber. The adverse weather almost doomed the crew. The two men took turns crawling onto the wings to chip away the ice. Sixteen hours after takeoff, the Vimy crash-landed in an Irish bog.

New Weapons

As glamorous as it may have seemed, air power did not play a key role in deciding the outcome of the war. With technologically new and innovative methods of inflicting destruction, the brutal and senseless fighting on the ground was far more instrumental.

The machine gun, invented by American **Hiram Maxim** in 1884, was widely used in World War I. U.S. troops used the Browning Automatic Rifle (**BAR**), first produced in 1892, after it entered the war. The lightweight automatic machine gun, developed by U.S. Army Colonel **Isaac Newton Lewis** in 1911, was often used on aircraft as well as in the trenches. Operating under the same principles as today's automatic weapons, the machine gun of World War I dominated combat during the long stalemate in the trenches with its awesome firepower.

Artillery was also a major factor in ground combat, especially after the introduction of high-explosive shells that could decimate large areas with their blasts and flying shrapnel. These shells now could be fired in rapid succession with the development of a field gun using recoil — the backward force produced by the firing of the projectile — to eject the empty shell casing. The French 75-millimeter cannon, considered by many to be the most effective artillery piece of the war, could fire 15 rounds a minute and remained in service until World War II.

The Germans used heavier guns than the Allies, with longer ranges and larger projectiles. Their **"Paris Gun"** had a barrel more than 100 feet long that launched 250-pound rounds over a record-breaking 75 miles. They shelled Paris with this weapon for 140 days in 1918. Germany's largest and most famous gun was **"Big Bertha"**, a 420-millimeter howitzer that fired a one-ton shell over a range of six miles. It was the world's largest cannon.

The mortar, a much smaller form of artillery, was also an effective weapon in trench warfare. This short-barreled weapon was used to fire relatively slow-moving projectiles at high-angle trajectories. **Wilfred Stokes** developed the modern three-inch mortar for the British Army during World War I.

Artillery's effectiveness was increased with the use of field radios, which provided instantaneous communication between commanders and troops. The gunner no longer had to be in view of his target. A distant observer, using a radio, could call in the exact target coordinates. Because telephones use wires, they are vulnerable to being cut by enemy patrols. Radio, therefore, played an integral role in warfare, and was used extensively for long-range communications.

Although high explosives were terrifying, the most dreaded weapons of the war were the chemicals. German chemist **Fritz Haber** developed a way to release poisonous chlorine from cylinders, forming a gas cloud that would blow over enemy lines. The Germans were the first to use chemical warfare on April 22, 1915, when they dropped 160 tons of liquid chlorine in nearly 6,000 pressurized canisters over Ypres, Belgium. The Allies were completely unprepared and suffered heavy casualties; 5,000 troops died and 10,000 were injured.

Haber then came up with his next chemical weapon, called phosgene, an asphyxiating gas with delayed effects. Then came mustard gas, which was even more brutal. It caused severe blisters on all body surfaces and remained on the ground and equipment to inflict casualties long after the initial attack. By the end of the war, artillery shells, mortars, and aerial bombs for both sides of the conflict were carrying these chemicals to their targets.

John Holland aboard the USS Holland submarine

A new invention called the **gas mask** provided a defense against chlorine and phosgene, but there was no way to defend against mustard gas. An African-American, **Garrett A. Morgan**, invented the mask, which he originally called the safety hood, in 1912. Once the mask is placed over the head, a tube releases exhaled air while another tube, lined with absorbent material, filters out harmful particles and provides fresh air.

Morgan's marketing attempts were initially unsuccessful, but after a 1916 explosion at the Cleveland Water Works trapped a group of workers in a tunnel under Lake Erie, Morgan arrived on the scene and proved his safety hood's usefulness. The heavy smoke and poison gas had prevented the workers' rescue until Morgan and three volunteers wearing gas masks went in and saved 32 lives. This event led to widespread publicity, and Morgan received an influx of orders for gas masks. Sadly, orders slowed down when they discovered that the inventor was black. Morgan then hired a white man to demonstrate the device as if he was the inventor.

Unaware of Morgan's invention, British troops were tying chemically treated cotton pads over their mouths and noses to protect themselves from poison-gas attacks. Eventually the news spread, and advanced masks with a charcoal filter based on Morgan's design soon began to be used in the war.

Yet another important new ground weapon of World War I was the **tank**. The purpose of the armored, tracked vehicle was to run over the thick barbed wire protecting the enemy's trenches, firing its machine gun as it passed, and clear the way for the infantry to advance. The design of the first tank, the British **Mark I**, was based on an agricultural tractor. Its rhomboid- shaped body housed an eight-man crew, four of whom were needed just to steer.

The British introduced their armored vehicle at the **Battle of the Somme** on September 15, 1916. Twenty Mark I tanks were deployed, but they were far less effective than anticipated. Many bogged down in the mud or became stuck in artillery-shell craters. The fundamental problem was the lack of appropriate strategy for the new weapon. The British finally used their tanks successfully at the **Battle of Cambrai** in November 1917. This time 216 tanks were used, and they served their purpose well by breaking through the fortified trenches and delivering the infantry to its target. Like the airplane, tanks did not have a major impact on this war. Both were new technologies that would eventually be far more critical in future conflicts.

The major naval innovation of the war was the submarine. Irish-American **John P. Holland** designed and built the first effective submarine, using an electric motor for underwater propulsion and a gasoline engine for surface movement. He sold the U.S. Navy its first underwater vessel, the U.S.S. Holland, in 1901, and licensed his design to the British company Vickers.

Germany was developing its own submarine at this time, and the first German U-boat (Unterseeboot), the **U-1**, was launched in 1906. Its main drawback was its kerosene-powered engine, which released a large cloud of white smoke and revealed the U-boat's presence. Prior to World War I, every major European power had assembled submarine fleets and was using diesel engines to propel them.

The Germans demonstrated the submarine's true potential on September 22, 1914, when a single U-boat sank three British armored cruisers within one hour. The British were stunned by the submarine's stealth and awesome destructive capability. The previously skeptical German High Command became convinced of the new weapon's usefulness.

In response to the superior British Royal Navy's blockade of their waters, the Germans decided to use their U-boats to sink merchant ships in British waters. On February 2, 1915, Germany declared "all the waters surrounding Great Britain and Ireland, including the English Channel, an area of war." This eventually led to the sinking of the British passenger liner, the **Lusitania**, by a German U-boat on May 7, 1915. Because 128 of the 1,198 dead passengers were American citizens, including famed writer Elbert Hubbard, there was massive public outcry in the United

States, which contributed to America's decision to enter the war in 1917.

To protect their ships from the marauding U-boats, the British developed depth charges. These canisters of high explosives, equivalent to 300 pounds of dynamite, would be triggered by increased water pressure and had a lethal radius of 25 feet, although the shock waves could inflict damage at much greater distances. Britain's best defense, however, proved to be its organization of ships into large, escorted convoys. This strategy dramatically limited the U-boats, effectiveness, and the submarines finally became little more than a nuisance to the British.

Peacetime Technology

Prior to the war, before German U-boats became a threat to British ships, the luxury liner **Titanic** had fallen victim to the powerful forces of nature. Proclaimed unsinkable by its owners and builders, the Titanic was considered by many to be the greatest ship afloat and a marvel of modern technology. The "great 15-story floating palace" was 882 feet long, and had all the modern amenities, including elevators, restaurants, theaters, bars, Turkish baths, swimming pools, tennis courts, and gardens. The Titanic embarked on its maiden voyage from England on April 9, 1912, with 2,224 passengers and crew. Five days later, it collided with a 50-foot-high iceberg. The unsinkable ship was suddenly sinking, and it carried only enough lifeboats for 1,178 people.

Like most ocean liners, the Titanic was equipped with Marconi radio equipment. It became the first ship to send wireless distress signals. A nearby ship responded to these SOS calls and arrived at the tragic scene within an hour to rescue the passengers lucky enough to have made it onto lifeboats. The survivors watched as the Titanic sank with its stern almost perpendicular to the icy Atlantic waters, taking 1,517 people with her—two-thirds of thos on board.

Radio technology received widespread publicity for the instrumental role it played in saving hundreds of lives in the Titanic disaster.

It was only a few months later that the next development in radio technology came. **Edwin H. Armstrong**, a student at Columbia University in New York, discovered a way to improve Lee De Forest's triode vacuum tube, the audion, and invented the **regenerative circuit**. Although it was an effective amplifier of electrical signals, the audion's flaw was its weak reception, and radio operators could listen to incoming transmissions only with headphones. Armstrong ran part of the triode's output current back into itself, which increased its sensitivity and amplified radio signals so they could be heard without earphones. Armstrong patented his invention in 1913, but De Forest challenged it in court. The two radio pioneers fought this legal battle for over 10 years until De Forest, backed by the American Telephone & Telegraph Company (AT&T), appealed to the U.S. Supreme Court and won on a technicality.

While serving in France during World War I, Armstrong made his second important discovery in 1917 with the invention of the **superheterodyne circuit**. Until that time, radio reception was a complicated procedure involving frequency adjustment for every stage of amplification. The superheterodyne receiver required just a turn of the dial to get good reception or to change the wavelength, making the radio accessible to the average person, rather than only to radio engineers. Radios soon spread into home use and became a medium for mass communications and entertainment. The superheterodyne circuit is still the standard in radio and television tuning.

Just as World War I was beginning in Europe, the **Panama Canal** opened after 10 years of construction. Built and controlled by the United States, the canal greatly shortened the long journey between America's two coasts by eliminating the need to sail around South America's southernmost tip at Cape Horn — a 7,000-mile difference.

The Panama Canal's history dates back to the 1880s when **Ferdinand de Lesseps**, the French engineer responsible for the Suez Canal, attempted to build a canal across the 50-mile wide Isthmus of Panama, which was then part of Colombia. The engineering difficulties, coupled with tropical diseases and harsh terrain, forced de Lesseps into bankruptcy in 1888, before he could complete half the canal.

Under President Theodore Roosevelt's leadership, the U.S. decided to try its hand at building the waterway, and began construction in 1904. The design called for a high-level canal utilizing a series of locks to raise and lower the water level, allowing ships to gradually ascend and descend through the isthmus. To accommodate this massive undertaking, 200 miles of railroad were built to move the excavated soil cut out of the ground from depths of up to 272 feet. The completed canal opened in August 1914, with a width of 300 feet and a minimum depth of 41 feet.

"Never before on our planet," said British scholar James Bryce, "have so much labor, so much scientific knowledge, and so much executive skill been concentrated on a work designed to bring the nations nearer to one another and serve the interests of all mankind."

With the opening of the Panama Canal, America's two distant coasts were brought closer. The widespread proliferation of automobiles, meanwhile, made it easier for people to travel over land, and advances in aviation allowed the commercial air-travel industry to take off. The world was indeed shrinking, but technological progress during the years of the Great War came at a high price.

TECHNOLOGY

chapter 3

1920-1929

The Birth of Broadcasting

First 5-kilowatt broadcast transmitter and receiver

As the world was recovering from the devastation of the Great War, technology created new forms of mass media and entertainment. The scars of the war could not be entirely healed, but these new diversions helped to ease the pain.

Although radio had been invented two decades earlier, it had been used primarily for private transmissions. Public broadcasting began in the United States in 1920, providing a new source of entertainment and news, and it quickly gained a large national audience. The new medium helped spread the popularity of jazz, a relatively new type of improvisational American music. The decade was to become known as the Jazz Age and the Roaring Twenties. Later, an invention called television began transmitting visual images and would add a whole new dimension to broadcasting. New entertainment innovations, such as movies with sound, or "talkies", transformed the motion-picture industry.

German airships began carrying civilian passengers in 1910, but that ceased during WWI, when air travel was used mainly for military purposes. The Twenties would see great growth in civil aviation as the airplane's capabilities were stretched to new limits and expanded uses. Looking past the skies and up to the stars, a misunderstood and often ridiculed visionary named Robert Goddard took a large step for mankind by inventing the modern rocket.

The war had left much of Europe in ruins — structurally, politically, and economically. The hardest hit were the defeated Germans, whose newly formed Weimar Republic found itself faced with harsh economic restrictions imposed by the Treaty of Versailles. In severe financial difficulty, Germany resorted to printing extra currency to make the reparation payments, which led to uncontrollable inflation.

In 1923, at a Munich beer garden, Adolf Hitler, a nationalist revolutionary, attempted to overthrow the government. This "Beer Hall Putsch" failed, and Hitler was sent to prison, where he wrote *Mein Kampf* (My Struggle), a book outlining his plans for building a new German empire.

Benito Mussolini became Europe's first fascist leader in 1922 when he took over an economically and politically unstable Italy. Mussolini established a totalitarian regime through his campaigns of terror and propaganda.

Also in 1922, Vladimir Lenin renamed the newly established communist state, formerly known as Russia, the Union of Soviet Socialist Republics (U.S.S.R.), also known as the Soviet Union. Lenin died in 1924, leaving Joseph Stalin and Leon Trotsky to compete for power. Stalin eventually exiled his rival in 1928, and took command of the nation. Determined to modernize the Soviet Union at any cost, Stalin exercised his totalitarian power to its fullest and did not hesitate to exterminate anyone suspected of dissension.

Hoping to ensure that the "war to end all wars" would live up to its name, U.S. Secretary of State Frank B. Kellogg and French Foreign Minister Aristide Briand proposed an agreement in 1928, known as the Kellogg-Briand Pact, to settle international disputes peacefully and outlaw war as an instrument of national policy. Almost every country in the world joined the ambitious pact, but it lacked any enforcement provisions and ultimately failed to prevent future conflicts.

Much of the world, meanwhile, was hopeful that the Great War had taught mankind a valuable lesson. Recognizing the mood of the country, U.S. President Warren G. Harding called for a "return to normalcy" in his 1920 campaign.

Tuning In

Many of the soldiers who returned home from the war had learned new skills in the service, and while firing a mortar was not very useful in civilian life, the ability to operate radio equipment was. Radio had proved its usefulness in the first two decades of the century, but it had not yet become the powerful communication tool that we know today. It had mainly served the same purpose as the telegraph — transmitting signals between two parties — but without wires. The closest things to

public broadcasts were transmitted by amateur radio operators, called **"hams"**, who sent news, weather, music, or whatever they desired over the airwaves. The only people receiving these signals, however, were other hams, many of whom had been trained in wireless communication during the war.

> **"While theoretically and technically television may be feasible, commercially and financially I consider it an impossibility, a development of which we need waste little time dreaming."**
>
> Lee de Forest, 1926

One of these hams was Westinghouse engineer **Frank Conrad**. After the war, he began transmitting music from his garage in Pittsburgh, PA, and received positive responses from other hams, some of whom were requesting their favorite songs. Word began to spread of Conrad's broadcasts, and soon people were buying receivers so they could listen.

The big companies dominating the radio industry at this time, such as Westinghouse, the Radio Corporation of America (RCA), and AT&T, were not concerned with public broadcasting; they did not initially see a way to make money in it. Instead they stuck to providing wireless telegraphy services, which enabled ship-to-shore communication.

Tommy guns

However, the interest in radio soon increased after Conrad's employers, at Westinghouse, learned of his growing on-air popularity. They suddenly realized that broadcasting inspired people to buy wireless receivers, and Westinghouse could build and sell them. Within a matter of weeks, Westinghouse set up a transmitting station in Pittsburgh and received a broadcasting license with the commercial call letters **KDKA**. On November 2, 1920, KDKA made the world's first scheduled commercial broadcast with coverage of the presidential election between Warren G. Harding and James M. Cox. The transmission made national news, and the radio industry almost instantly turned its attention to broadcasting.

At that time, those companies involved in broadcasting made most of their money by manufacturing and selling radio receivers. Others soon discovered that there was money to be made from broadcasting alone. An outbreak of new broadcasting stations in the U.S. followed, and the number of receivers in homes skyrocketed. In 1922, less than 1 percent of American homes owned radio sets; the number had risen to 60 percent by 1932. Radio was more than a national fad; it was a kind of obsession. Twenty million people listened to the 1924 presidential election on more than 400 stations. While listening to the 1927 broadcast of the heavyweight championship fight between Jack Dempsey and Gene Tunney, 10 fans reportedly died of excitement. In the 1920s, radio broadcasting became the fastest-growing industry in America.

Experimental station 2XB, NYC

Broadcasting companies began looking for new ways to expand their profits. When the idea of selling time for advertisements had been introduced, most people disapproved, including Secretary of Commerce Herbert Hoover, the future president, whose office governed radio licensing.

"It is inconceivable that we should allow so great a possibility for service, for news, for entertainment, for education to be drowned in advertising chatter," Hoover said in 1922.

John Baird, television pioneer

Despite Hoover's opposition, it didn't take long for advertising to become an integral part of broadcasting.

AT&T entered broadcasting in 1922 with its radio station **WEAF** in New York City. Since the company did not sell radio equipment, it needed another way to make money in this venture. AT&T's strategy was to operate its radio station like a telephone service, but to large audiences; for a fee, it would allow anyone who wanted to transmit a message or entertain the audience to use the studio. AT&T provided only the facilities, not the content — just like a telephone. In between these paid time slots, WEAF broadcast entertaining events, such as stage shows, concerts, and sports, which attracted large audiences and compelled businesses to advertise on the air. The first commercial aired on August 28, 1922, and by the end of the decade the radio industry was making most of its money from advertising.

These developments in the radio industry were made possible by past technical innovations, but the triode, the main element in a radio receiver, still had a flaw: As it amplified the incoming signal, it also amplified the distortion.

American **Harold S. Black**, an electrical engineer for Bell Telephone Laboratories, discovered a way to reduce distortion in 1923. By subtracting the amplitude of the output signal from that of the input signal, the two signals would cancel each other out and leave only the distortion. The distortion could then be amplified and fed back, thus canceling out the original distortion. This "feedback-feedforward" system reduced distortion, but failed to eliminate it, so Black continued his research.

He was crossing the Hudson River on a ferry when the solution came to him. Black wrote down his thoughts and worked out the necessary mathematical equations. By feeding the output signal of the amplifier back into the system negatively, or out of phase, he could theoretically reduce distortion indefinitely. In 1927 the **negative feedback amplifier** became a reality and the industry standard for distortion reduction in radio and telephone reception.

New Dimensions

Once radio transmission of audio was established, the next step for broadcasting was to transmit images. The idea dates back to 1884, when German engineer **Paul Nipkow** invented a mechanical system of scanning images, called the Nipkow disk. It was a metal or cardboard disk with a series of holes spiraling toward the center of the disk. Placed between the subject and a strong light, the rapidly rotating disk scanned the image through each passing hole as a series of lines stacked on top of one another. Nipkow had the right idea, but the technology was not available at the time to turn it into a working television system; that would happen 40 years later.

After failing at several businesses, and unable to continue with his engineering job at an electrical company because of poor health, Scotsman **John L. Baird** began experimenting with Nipkow's television system in 1922. Working under the constraints of poverty, Baird used household objects to build a television in his London attic.

"Scanning discs were cut out of cardboard," his friend Ronald Tiltman wrote, "and the mountings consisted of darning needles and old scrap timber."

Along with the Nipkow disk, Baird employed a photoelectric cell, which used the photosensitive metal selenium to read the varying degrees of light from the image and convert them into electrical impulses. He used another Nipkow disk for playback, synchronized with a flashing light bulb, whose brightness depended on the signals from the photoelectric cell.

In 1924 Baird transmitted a small flickering image of a Maltese cross more than 10 feet across his attic. The wide pink stripes made it hardly recognizable, but it was a working transmission of an image. He continued to improve the system, and in 1925 Gordon Selfridge offered Baird the opportunity to demonstrate the invention in his department store.

Baird's television system was an instant success at Selfridge's, attracting long lines of people three times a day to see a transmitted image of the world's first star of the small screen: a ventriloquist's dummy named Bill.

FIRST TELEVISION CAMERA

USA

Philo T. Farnsworth

20c

Stamp commemorating Philip T. Farnsworth

Scotch Tape

Many of the cars on the road in the Twenties had two-tone paint jobs, as was the style. This presented a problem for the auto painters: In order to produce a clean line between the two colors, they had to mask the first color painted by fastening paper over that part of the body when painting the second color. Unfortunately, all the glues and adhesive tapes available were so sticky that they peeled some of the paint off when removed.

In 1925 a technician at the Minnesota Mining & Manufacturing Company (now called 3M), Richard Drew, developed a pressure-sensitive adhesive tape that did not damage paint. Because it was less sticky, it could also now be easily dispensed from a roll.

The two-inch-wide tape was originally manufactured with two thin strips of adhesive running down the length of its edges. Minnesota Mining & Manufacturing reasoned that this would be sufficient, for one edge would hold the paper, and the other would stick to the body. The masking paper, however, was too heavy for such a small amount of adhesive and often pulled the tape off. According to company legend, an irritated painter told a company salesman, "Take this tape back to your stingy Scotch bosses and tell them to put more adhesive on it." The term "Scotch" refers to the reputation of the Scottish people for frugality. Rather than being offended by such a remark, the bosses decided to adopt the term as their brand name, and they took the painter's advice; from then on, they covered the entire surface of Scotch tape with glue.

Scotch masking tape solved auto painting problems

Wanting to televise a living person, Baird paid an office boy named William Taynton to step behind the camera, making Taynton the first professional TV star.

After three weeks at Selfridge's, Baird threw a demonstration party and invited 40 members of the prestigious Royal Society of London for the Improving of Natural Knowledge. Arriving in full evening dress, the guests were impressed with Baird's presentation, and the next day's London Times reported the event. Suddenly the previously impoverished Baird was famous and receiving financial support from investors for his research.

With his newfound funding, Baird began experimenting with images transmitted through telephone lines, and in 1927 he successfully sent a television signal 430 miles from London to Glasgow. He topped this feat in 1928 with a trans-Atlantic transmission from London to New York. Impressed with this achievement, the New York Times praised Baird as an innovator in the same league with Guglielmo Marconi.

"All the more remarkable is Baird's achievement because he matches his inventive wits against the pooled ability and the vast resources of the great corporate physicists and engineers, thus far with dramatic success," the Times stated.

The **BBC** (British Broadcasting Corporation), founded in 1922 as Britain's public radio broadcasting service, decided to use Baird's system for an experimental television broadcast on September 30, 1929. The broadcast, viewed on one of Baird's television receivers called a **"televisor"**, consisted of an announcer reading a letter on the screen, and a speech by vacuum-tube inventor John A. Fleming.

Although he continued to improve his device, Baird's transmission still had a very low resolution — a flaw that could not be fully corrected with a spinning disk system. While Baird was devoting himself to the mechanical design, two inventors working independently in the United States were developing fully electronic systems that would eventually make Baird's televisor obsolete.

Philo T. Farnsworth had been interested in electronics as a boy growing up in Utah and had read about Nipkow's disk system. When he was 15 years old, Farnsworth told his high school teacher about a better television system he had devised that did not rely on Nipkow disks, and he drew the plans for the electronic apparatus on the blackboard. Impressed by the boy's ingenuity, the teacher encouraged him to build it.

After securing some financial backers, Farnsworth moved to California and began his research in secrecy. In 1927 he had a working machine with which he transmitted a series of images. It was crude, but the **"image dissector"** was a working electronic television system. Farnsworth applied for a patent and continued to improve it.

Around the same time, Russian immigrant **Vladimir Zworykin** was also working on an electronic television device. He had moved to the United States in 1919, and soon found work as an engineer for Westinghouse.

In 1923 Zworykin applied for a patent for what he claimed to be the first electronic television camera, called the **"iconoscope"**. It used thousands of tiny droplets of selenium, each acting as a photoelectric cell. As light from the subject passed through the lens, each droplet generated a different electric charge depending on the brightness of the light to which it was exposed. The iconoscope then quickly scanned these impulses, collected the series of images, and ran them together to produce the illusion of motion.

A year later he applied for another patent; this time it was for a television receiver called a **kinescope**, which converted the signal back into a visual image on a fluorescent screen. An integral element of the kinescope was a **cathode-ray tube** (CRT). Invented in 1897 by German **Ferdinand Braun** to help him study electrical impulses, it produced an image on a fluorescent screen by passing a beam of electrons through an electromagnetic field. It was the predecessor of today's picture tube.

Zworykin's superiors at Westinghouse were less than enthusiastic with his results. The crude iconoscope produced a hazy, unclear picture, and they didn't see any reason to improve it. Zworykin continued his research, and presented a modified system to the executives at Westinghouse in 1929. It was still far from perfect, and again they were not impressed.

By this time, Zworykin's developments had caught the eye of **David Sarnoff**, the head of RCA. Sarnoff was one of a handful of industry executives with the foresight to recognize the potential of television. He had told his board of directors in 1923 that someday he expected every household in America to have a television set that "will make it possible for those at home to see as well as hear what is going on in the studio."

Sarnoff, also a Russian immigrant, hired Zworykin as RCA's director of research in 1929. In that nurturing environment, Zworykin began perfecting the iconoscope/kinescope system.

The stage was being set for a battle to be fought in the next decade between Farnsworth and Zworykin — the modest resources of the independent inventor versus the unlimited means of the corporate research laboratory.

You Ain't Heard Nothing Yet

Meanwhile, just as the broadcasting industry was learning to add visuals to its audio, the motion-picture industry was doing the opposite — that is, adding audio to its visuals.

In the early days of cinema, movie houses often had live pianists playing soundtracks to silent films, but this added only music, not voices. Some houses attempted to play a phonograph record of the spoken word along with the film, but it was difficult to synchronize the two. Just a slight difference in speed between them often made the experience unpleasant.

ELECTRIC RAZOR

Hoping to find a way to shave without covering the surface of his face with soap and water, retired U.S. Army colonel Jacob Schick mortgaged his house in Connecticut after World War I to finance the enterprise. He managed to come up with an electric razor that used a series of slots to hold the hairs in place while an array of moving blades shaved them off. Patented in 1928, it was the first successful electric razor. Other companies released competing models shortly afterward, but they were all variations of Schick's design.

Lee De Forest began working on the problem of synchronizing sound with motion pictures in 1919, and came up with an effective method of recording the audio directly onto the film as an electronic code. A special projector then converted the code back into sound and amplified it through loudspeakers. He gave a demonstration of his invention, called **Phonofilm**, to movie industry executives in 1923, but they did not see a need for it. It was expensive, and silent movies were doing well enough at the box office. They didn't want to risk fixing something they felt was not broken.

One company, however, was willing to take the chance with sound. At the time, Warner Brothers was a small movie studio, and its executives decided to make a film with sound, but not with De Forest's system. Instead, they chose to record the audio onto a phonograph record with an improved process developed by the Vitaphone Company. The first movie to include the audible human voice was *The Jazz Singer*, featuring superstar Al Jolson. The soundtrack was to consist only of music and singing, but after finishing a song one day, Jolson unexpectedly improvised a brief monologue. "Wait a minute. Wait a minute," he said. "You ain't heard nothing yet!"

Warner Brothers released *The Jazz Singer* in 1927, and although only about 100 movie theaters in the U.S. had sound capabilities, it was a big success. The film proved that a huge market existed for talking movies, and launched the age of the **"talkies."**

The following year, Warner Brothers released *Lights of New York*, the first complete talkie. The $23,000 movie made $1,252,000 at the box office. It quickly became clear that talkies were no novelty and that they were here to stay.

"Moving pictures need sound as much as Beethoven symphonies need lyrics," film superstar Charlie Chaplin had said, but the talkie revolution could not be stopped, and it quickly rendered silent movies obsolete.

By this time, De Forest's Phonofilm had stirred up interest. It proved to be a better way to synchronize the sound with the action, compared with the Vitaphone. After RCA introduced the system in 1928 it quickly became the industry standard. By 1930, 95 percent of all new major films were talkies, and almost half the movie houses in the U.S. and one-third in the world were wired for sound.

A Star in the Sky

One of the biggest stars of the Twenties found his fame not on the big screen, but in the open skies. Twenty-

five-year-old American pilot **Charles A. Lindbergh** became a national hero in 1927 after becoming the first person to fly non-stop from New York to Paris in the first solo flight across the Atlantic.

Prior to his historic flight, Lindbergh was an airmail pilot for the U.S. Post Office, which by this time had extended its operations from coast to coast. Flying the mail was a challenging and dangerous job in the early days. The courageous pilots, often flying in adverse weather and open cockpits, needed to be excellent navigators as well as mechanics, for their planes often needed repairs during missions. After an engine failure forced him to crash, pilot Dean Smith sent the following message: "On trip 4 westbound. Flying low. Engine quit. Only place to land on cow. Killed cow. Wrecked plane. Scared me. Smith."

These poor flying conditions led to many problems and fatalities. The Post Office hired its first 40 pilots in 1918, and only nine of those were still alive by 1925.

To help with aviation navigation, President Warren G. Harding authorized the installation of a system of flashing beacons on the ground along flight paths nationwide. These beacons and several emergency landing fields were installed by 1924. At the time, airmail took 33 hours to reach New York from San Francisco.

Looking for a new challenge, Lindbergh decided to try to win the **Orteig Prize**, whose sponsors offered $25,000 to whoever completed the first non-stop flight between New York and Paris. The 3,600-mile route was nearly twice as far as the one taken by Alcock and Brown in their flight from Newfoundland to Ireland in 1919. Because of the amount of fuel needed to complete such a long flight, a major problem was simply lifting off the ground with so much weight. Several renowned World War I pilots with their crews had already crashed and died attempting the flight before Lindbergh took his turn. Compared to these men, the young Lindbergh was a nobody, and the only one who proposed to fly alone. Considered crazy, he had trouble finding a sponsor and an aircraft company to build him a plane.

Lindbergh finally secured sponsorship from the *St. Louis Globe-Democrat* newspaper and from some local businessmen hoping to promote their city. The investors named the future aircraft **The Spirit of St. Louis**. The Ryan Aircraft Company of San Diego, also relatively unknown, agreed to work with Lindbergh on modifying one of its planes to carry extra fuel for the long journey. They placed a large fuel tank in front of the cockpit, which obstructed the pilot's forward view. Lindbergh didn't think this would be a problem, since there was not much to see over the expanse of the Atlantic Ocean. The only way to see out of the plane were from the side windows and a retractable periscope. Worried about extra weight, he also refused to carry a radio. Lindbergh took off from New York on the rainy morning of May 20, 1927.

"*The Spirit of St. Louis* feels more like an overloaded truck than an airplane," he wrote in his log.

Staying awake for more than 33 hours was difficult for Lindbergh, and he dozed several times, with nearly disastrous consequences. When he finally landed in Paris, the welcoming party was large enough to cause the biggest traffic jam in French history. As the people broke through police lines and rushed toward the landing plane, Lindbergh turned off his propeller to keep from harming them.

Lindbergh was suddenly a hero and a world-famous celebrity. President Calvin Coolidge sent a Navy ship to bring him home, and nearly four million people cheered him in the streets of Manhattan during his ticker-tape parade.

Charles Lindbergh refueling the Spirit of St. Louis

"In the spring of '27 something bright and alien flashed across the sky," author F. Scott Fitzgerald wrote. "A young Minnesotan who seemed to have nothing to do with his generation did a heroic thing, and for a moment people set down their glasses in country clubs and speakeasies and thought of their old best dreams."

Rocket Man

Robert Goddard, and his rocket, 1925

Since a child growing up in Boston, **Robert H. Goddard** had dreamed of manned space flight. Inspired by H.G. Wells' novel *The War of the Worlds*, he dedicated his life to making these dreams come true. Goddard received a doctorate in physics from Clark University in 1911, and subsequently wrote a treatise published by the Smithsonian Institution called *A Method of Reaching Extreme Altitudes*. Goddard proposed the use of rockets powered by liquid fuel to escape the Earth's atmosphere.

The concept of rockets was nothing new. Invented in China, centuries before, rockets propelled by gunpowder had been used for fireworks, but they were unreliable, inefficient, and not very powerful. Goddard believed that a combination of gasoline and liquid oxygen would deliver more thrust and prove to be a better power source.

He was not the first person with such an idea. In *Research into Interplanetary Space by Means of Rocket Power*, published in 1903, Russian school teacher **Konstantin Tsiolkovsky** advocated the use of liquid-propelled rockets to travel into space. He also described the use of multi-stage rockets, by which sections are discarded after use to reduce weight while leaving Earth's atmosphere. Many of his principles were later adopted and used today in actual space flights.

While Tsiolkovsky merely postulated theories, Goddard turned them into reality. On March 16, 1926, at his aunt's farm at Auburn, Massachusetts, Goddard became the first person to successfully launch a liquid-propelled rocket. Launched from a frame made of water pipes, the four-foot-tall projectile flew to an altitude of 41 feet at 60 miles per hour.

Goddard's successes would eventually change the course of history, but few people realized it at the time. In fact, most considered the noisy experiments a public nuisance. He launched another larger rocket carrying meteorological equipment in 1929. After his second launch, the state fire marshal ordered him not to do it again.

Fortunately for Goddard, the publicity from this fiasco attracted the attention of Charles Lindbergh. The famous aviator used his influence to raise funding for Goddard's work. During the next decade Goddard would continue his tests in remote Roswell, New Mexico, where he set up the world's first professional rocket-testing facility. By 1935 he was launching rockets traveling faster than the speed of sound up to altitudes of 8,000 feet. He also began using gyroscopes to stabilize the rockets and control their course. In his isolated desert station, Goddard perfected many of the fundamental principles used in modern rockets.

Knocking Out the Knock

Meanwhile, back on planet Earth, people were more concerned with ordinary terrestrial transportation. Powered by liquid fuel, automobiles were limited in their performance by the common problem of engine knock, a metallic knocking or pinging sound caused by an engine that it is not burning fuel efficiently. A gasoline's octane number is a measure of its resistance to knocking. In 1921 a

An early refinery engineer

team of American chemists led by **Thomas Midgley Jr.** and **T. A. Boyd**, at General Motors, discovered that a small amount of tetraethyl lead added to a car's gasoline prevented knock and raised the engine's octane rating. This allowed car manufacturers to improve performance by building engines with higher internal pressures. It would later be discovered, however, that lead released poisonous compounds into the air when it is burned, causing environmental pollution.

As roads for automobiles continued to be laid down in industrialized nations, a new kind of roadway was introduced in the 1920s: the limited-access highway. Its purpose was to allow the free flow of traffic by eliminating intersections.

The construction of the first such highway began in Berlin in 1909, but Germany's involvement in World War I delayed its completion. The 6.25-mile **Avus Autobahn** finally opened in 1921, utilizing 10 overpasses for cross- traffic. In Italy, the Milan-to-Varese **Autostrada** opened in 1924, and one year later America's first freeway, the 15.5-mile **Bronx River Parkway**, was completed north of New York City.

With improved transportation and new forms of entertainment such as radio and talking movies, the Twenties had reason to roar. New technologies and new heroes created out of peacetime offered hope for the future, but the world was about to enter one of its darkest chapters in its history.

1930's Service Station

TECHNOLOGY

chapter 4

1930-1939
Television Wars
and
Radio Defenses

Stan Livingston and Earnest Lawrence with 27" cyclotron

When the U.S. stock market crashed on October 29, 1929, the Roaring Twenties came to a screeching halt. Known as Black Tuesday, that day marked the beginning of the Great Depression, which lasted throughout the 1930s. It was the worst economic recession in the nation's history and it quickly spread to the rest of the world.

Promising a "New Deal" to help America's economy, Democrat Franklin Delano Roosevelt won the presidency by a landslide from incumbent Herbert Hoover in 1932. By the time Roosevelt was inaugurated the following year, the national unemployment rate had reached almost 24 percent. In his first 100 days of office, the new president signed numerous New Deal laws that created various federally supported economic recovery programs such as the National Recovery Administration, the Federal Emergency Relief Administration, and the Tennessee Valley Authority.

BALLPOINT PEN

More common than computers and photocopiers in offices, the ballpoint pen was invented in 1938 by the Hungarian brothers Ladislao and Georg Biro. To escape the rapidly spreading Nazi regime, the brothers emigrated to Buenos Aires, Argentina, in 1940. After improving the design, they patented it in 1943. Englishman Henry Martin had met the inventors the same year and acquired the British rights for their invention. The first ballpoint pens were manufactured in England in 1944 for the Royal Air Force; they were the only pens that worked at high altitudes.

Using the radio, on March 12, 1933, Roosevelt addressed the nation in the first of a long and successful series of "fireside chats". The broadcasts' intimate quality made listeners feel as though the president was sitting in the room with them.

In another powerful use of radio, actor/producer Orson Welles' Halloween 1938 radio broadcast based on the H.G. Wells novel, *War of the Worlds*, caused widespread panic, as listeners were fooled into believing that Earth was being attacked by invaders from Mars.

Realistic as it may have sounded, the world was not being invaded by interplanetary aliens. A series of real invasions, however, would soon force Earthlings into a second world war.

The decade's first major invasion came in 1931 when Japan overran the Chinese province of Manchuria, sparking the Sino-Japanese War. Throughout the decade, Chiang Kai-shek and his communist rival, Mao Tse-tung, battled for power in China while the nation was at war with Japan.

In Germany, Adolf Hitler's National Socialist (Nazi) Party became that nation's largest party by 1932. Hitler was appointed chancellor of Germany in 1933, and quickly established himself as dictator. Calling himself the Führer, or leader, he set out to return his country to its former glory. Hitler blamed the Jewish population for Germany's downfall, and in 1935 he promulgated the Nuremberg Laws, which stripped Jews of their citizenship and civil rights. After denouncing the Treaty of Versailles, Hitler began rebuilding Germany's armed forces and, contrary to the terms of the treaty, sent his troops into the demilitarized Rhineland, a region in Germany bordering France.

Following Germany's lead, Austria became a dictatorship under Engelbert Dollfuss in 1934; he was later assassinated by the Nazis. Benito Mussolini's fascist army invaded Ethiopia in 1935, causing much of Europe and America to change its positive opinion of Italy. The Spanish Civil War broke out in 1936 as General Francisco Franco's fascist forces rebelled against the newly elected left-wing government. With the help of Germany and Italy, Franco was victorious in 1939.

In 1938 Hitler annexed his native Austria and allied Germany with Italy and Japan, forming the Axis powers. To avoid war with Germany, Great Britain and France, the Allies, adopted a policy of appeasement, hoping Hitler would be satisfied if they let him have what he wanted. Hitler was not appeased, and later that year the Allies agreed to let him annex Czechoslovakia's Sudetenland, which had a large German population, in exchange for his promise not to further expand his borders.

Germany was preparing for war, and signed a non-aggression pact with the Soviet Union in August 1939 to avoid a conflict on two fronts. Armed with a strong modern army, Hitler invaded Poland on September 1. Using a new strategy called "blitzkrieg" (lightning war), which incorporated dive bombers, tanks, and infantry into quick and powerful strikes. The Germans quickly conquered Poland, and two days later, the Allies declared war on Germany.

The decade of the thirties, which started with a worldwide depression ended with a world at war. Because of, and in spite of these trying times, technology progressed. Britain's secret development of radar played an instrumental role in repelling Hitler's invasion of the island nation and changed the course of the war. In the United States, Philo Farnsworth and Vladimir Zworykin spent most of the decade engaged in a war of their own over the development of the world's first successful television system.

The Television Drama

Before Zworykin accepted the job at RCA, he told RCA president David Sarnoff that it might cost about $100,000 to perfect his electronic system. As it turned out, Sarnoff and RCA would end up spending $50 million. In order to achieve their goal they had to deal with Philo Farnsworth's invention of the image dissector.

> **"Television? The word is half Latin and half Greek. No good can come of it."**
>
> C.P. Scott, (1932)

Although Zworykin applied for a patent in 1923, it took 15 years for the Patent Office to provide protection for his iconoscope. Meanwhile, Farnsworth received a patent for his image dissector in 1930. It was a different and somewhat better apparatus than Zworykin's. Seeing Farnsworth's progress as a threat and foreseeing possible patent infringement problems in the future, Sarnoff offered to buy Farnsworth out. Farnsworth, however, had other ideas. He knew he had something Sarnoff needed and turned down the offer. Anticipating television's future success, he wanted to negotiate a deal that would pay him royalties instead of one lump sum.

Sarnoff was outraged. RCA had never

Vladimir Zworykin with iconoscope

Farnsworth, Zworykin was busy working in the laboratory, and in 1933 he had a major breakthrough, resulting in a highly improved iconoscope. By making the photoelectric cells smaller, he could now fit one million of them into the camera and greatly improve the resolution. He informed Sarnoff that it was ready for public use, and they arranged for an experimental broadcast. RCA successfully transmitted images over a distance of four miles to a nine-inch picture tube.

Shortly after coming to terms with Farnsworth, RCA displayed its new electronic television system as the centerpiece of its Exhibition Hall at the **New York World's Fair** in 1939. Priced at $625 per set, it was well out of financial reach for most people; food and shelter seemed to be a higher priority in the aftermath of the Great Depression. RCA also did not yet have a commercial broadcasting license for television.

Across the Atlantic, John Baird improved his mechanical television by replacing the spinning Nipkow disk with a drum full of mirrors to scan images. He knew the fully electronic systems were gaining ground quickly and hoped to establish his system first. One thousand people had bought his televisor sets, and he was broadcasting a regular show on the BBC every night at 11 o'clock.

Baird tried to persuade the BBC, which controlled British broadcasting, to adopt his system as its standard. Unfortunately for Baird, it was becoming clear

before paid royalties to anyone, and he was hesitant to start. The company initially refused, hoping he would give in, but the tough-minded Farnsworth did not budge. They then began negotiations that would last a decade, and in 1939 RCA finally agreed to pay him royalties. Legend has it that the RCA attorney had tears in his eyes when he signed the contract with Farnsworth.

During the lengthy negotiations with

> **"(Television) won't be able to hold onto any market it captures after the first six months. People will soon get tired of staring at a plywood box every night."**
>
> Darryl F. Zanuck

that the American's electronic television produced higher-quality images than his mechanical counterpart. British companies were developing electronic systems of their own by this time. Electric and Musical Industries (EMI) patented an improved camera with higher resolution, called the **Emitron**, in 1932, to be used with the company's advanced picture tube. The Emitron, like other electronic cameras, was much more sensitive to light than the mechanical scanning system of Baird's.

Baird was already a national hero for his pioneering efforts in television, but the EMI system seemed to work better. However, the BBC decided to give both a chance. In 1936 it began broadcasting one week of Baird's mechanical system followed by one week of EMI's electronic system. The two alternated every week for three months. Although Baird's picture was impressive, it couldn't compete with EMI's resolution, and the BBC adopted the EMI system, which remained in use until 1964.

Shortly after making its decision, World War II had started, and television technology was deprioritized. The BBC completely suspended television broadcasting until war's end. Only then would it begin to make an impact as an important medium for mass communications.

Killer Waves

Radio, unlike its cousin, television, was already well established, but the amplitude-modulated (**AM**) signals, which were the only ones used for broadcasting, were susceptible to static interference by thunderstorms and electrical appliances.

1939 World's Fair gallery of Arts & Science

In 1933 **Edwin H. Armstrong**, inventor of the regenerative circuit and the superheterodyne circuit, made his third major contribution to radio technology by discovering a way to modulate the frequency of a signal's wavelength, rather than its amplitude. The frequency modulation (**FM**) system produced a much cleaner, static-free sound and would eventually make stereophonic broadcasts possible.

Despite improved broadcast quality, the radio industry did not welcome Armstrong's innovation with open arms. Instead, it considered it to be a potential competitor and a threat to the established AM broadcasters. Under industry pressure, the Federal Communications

1930's rectifier to change AC to DC

battles on behalf of her husband and eventually won them all.

New uses were also being developed for the radio wave, which proved vital in the shaping of history. Since the early days of radio, researchers and broadcasters began to notice that metallic objects reflected the transmitted waves. Various scientists, working independently, had reasoned that this phenomenon could be incorporated into some sort of detection system for ships and aircraft. These were the first steps in the development of **radar**, an acronym for Radio Detection and Ranging.

Commission (FCC) did not grant Armstrong an FM broadcasting permit until 1940.

Armstrong had sold the patent rights for his previous inventions in the 1920s, and by now was a wealthy man. Unable to find corporate support for his latest breakthrough, he spent $300,000 of his own money in 1939 to build the first FM broadcasting facility.

After the end of World War II, broadcasting companies began using FM to transmit television signals, but they were doing it without Armstrong's patent rights. Legal action followed, and fighting against corporate resources was a long and expensive process. Armstrong was nearly broke by the early 1950s, and his lawyers told him the lawsuits could very well last another decade.

The dejected Armstrong could take no more. In 1954 he threw himself from the window of his Manhattan apartment. His widow, Marion, continued the legal

As the threat of war intensified in the late 1930s, nations began preparing themselves for the inevitable. It was a widespread belief that aerial bombing would be a major factor in the next war; therefore, it became necessary to establish effective defenses against enemy air strikes. Great Britain, the favorite target of German bombers during World War I, felt especially threatened by the modern German air force, or **Luftwaffe**. The British were determined to find a suitable defense as quickly as possible.

The British Air Ministry initially attempted to use radio science to develop a "death ray," which would use radio waves to destroy enemy bombers by heating them to extreme temperatures. Unsuccessful in this endeavor, the Air Ministry appointed Britain's leading radio authority, Scottish physicist **Robert**

Watson-Watt, as its scientific advisor.

Watson-Watt was no stranger to radar. In 1919 he had patented the concept of **"echolocation"**. The term means locating objects with sound, which is how bats "see" in the dark, but Watson-Watt proposed using radio waves rather than sound waves. Because radio waves travel at a constant velocity — the same speed as light waves — the distance of an object can be determined by measuring the time it takes the signal to bounce back to its source. All this would be useless, however, if there was no way to visualize this information, so Watson-Watt added a cathode-ray tube (CRT), like the one used by Zworykin for his television screen, to display the exact position of the aircraft.

On February 26, 1935, the top-secret system was ready for a test. As a British bomber flew through a BBC radio transmission, Watson-Watt and his team saw a green dot appear on their monitor. The system had a range of only 10 miles, but it worked. The range would soon be increased.

"Britain has become an island once more," Watson-Watt said, recalling the reaction to Louis Blériot's flight three decades earlier.

A major improvement came the following year. Watson-Watt began using pulsed signals rather than the previously used continuous waves. The improved radar could now not only detect an object's presence, but also pinpoint its location. By 1938 Britain had installed a network of radio stations to protect the island with the invisible waves.

The final piece of the puzzle came into place in 1939, when **John T. Randall** and **Henry A. Boot** invented the **"multicavity magnetron"**, a microwave transmitting device. These extra-short waves made radar operation effective under any weather conditions and could be used with much smaller antennae, making portable radar possible.

The system was completed just in time. World War II started the same year, and after conquering France, Adolf Hitler began bombing England in July 1940. Outnumbered four to one in pilots and planes, the Royal Air Force (RAF) fought back and, with the help of its top-secret radar, won the **Battle of Britain**.

SCR-584, the first automatic tracking radar

Radar enabled the British to detect the German planes from distances of up to 150 miles, and the RAF effectively used their fighters to intercept the enemy bombers. When the Nazis resorted to night bombing, British fighter pilots used their on-board radar to help shoot them down.

1933 Boeing 247 commercial airplane

"We had nothing like it," Luftwaffe General Adolf Galland later said of the British radar system, which German pilots called "superbinoculars."

Radar was no death ray, but it proved to be the deciding factor in the Battle of Britain, a major turning point in World War II and world history.

Although it was originally created for military purposes, radar would later be used for predicting weather, exploring surfaces of other planets, measuring the speed of traffic, and navigation for aircraft, ships, rockets, and satellites.

The Fall of Airships and the Rise of Helicopters

Airplanes had replaced Zeppelins as bombers in World War I, but dirigibles remained the primary vehicle for civil air transportation between the world wars. Britain and Germany built improved airships and operated passenger services after the Great War, but the German Zeppelins remained the most famous and successful.

The **Graf Zeppelin**, one of the most famous airships, made its maiden voyage in 1928. It offered the most luxurious service of its time for 20 passengers, each paying between $1,000 and $3,000 to cross the Atlantic. Although the Graf Zeppelin carried a total of more than 13,000 passengers across the Atlantic in 144 flights without incident, other airships were not as fortunate. The first disaster occured in 1921, when the British dirigible R34, which had made the first trans-Atlantic round-trip flight in 1919, broke up and killed 40 people. Other disastrous accidents followed. The most famous was the May 6, 1937, explosion of the Zeppelin **Hindenburg**, the largest dirigible ever built, as it was preparing to land at Lakehurst, New Jersey.

"It's burning, bursting into flames and is falling on the mooring mast," a tearful announcer Herbert Morrison said in the coast-to-coast radio broadcast. "This is one of the worst catastrophes in the world...oh, the humanity and all the passengers."

Thirty-five of the 97 people on board

died as the flaming mass fell to the ground. The era of the passenger airship was over; lighter-than-air craft were retired from service soon after.

The job of air transport would now fall on the shoulders (or wings) of airplanes. Heavier-than-air craft had already been in use for these purposes, but airlines were finding it difficult to make a profit from passenger service alone, and, in the U.S., generally had to supplement their revenues by carrying mail for the Post Office.

In 1936 a new American airplane changed the industry. Because of its reliability and economical performance, the twin-engine **Douglas DC-3** suddenly made passenger airline travel profitable without the additional burden of mail delivery. The revolutionary monoplane could carry 21 passengers and became the industry standard both domestically and abroad. By 1938, 95 percent of American airline passengers were flying on DC-3s. Adapted for military use as the C-47, it was the primary transport plane in World War II for the United States as well as Great Britain. The DC-3, built until 1946 and reproduced around the world, is still flown today and has become the most widely used plane ever made.

After decades of development, an entirely different type of flying machine, called the **helicopter**, finally evolved into a successful design. The advantages of a helicopter over an airplane are its abilities to take off vertically and to hover, unlike an airplane, which has to be constantly moving forward to stay airborne.

The helicopter concept dates back to 14th century China, where flying toys were made with four propeller-like rotors attached to a shaft with string

wrapped around it. Pulling the string caused the rotors to spin and propel the toy into the air. In the 16th century, **Leonardo da Vinci** also had the idea and drew sketches of a flying machine using similar principles.

French engineer **Paul Cornu** achieved the first manned helicopter flight in 1907, but he rose only about one foot off the ground and remained in the air for 20 seconds. Early helicopter designers' main obstacle to sustained flight was the problem of torque: the spinning overhead rotor caused the body of the craft to rotate in the opposite direction. To counteract the torque, many designers used two propellers spinning in opposite directions. Cornu's machine had rotors mounted at both the front and rear.

Two years later in Russia, **Igor Sikorsky** built helicopters with two rotors on top of each other, and although they flew, they lacked the power to lift the additional weight of a pilot. The discouraged Sikorsky turned his attention to designing and building airplanes. In 1913 he built the **Bolshoi**, the world's first airplane with four engines, and supplied Russia with bombers based on this design during World War I. After the Russian Revolution, Sikorsky moved to New York and eventually started the Sikorsky Aero Corporation. He continued to build airplanes, but in the 1930s he once again began to concentrate on helicopters.

Others were also building helicopters around this time. Using a configuration similar to Sikorsky's early experiments utilizing two rotors stacked on top of each other, Frenchmen **Louis Bréguet** and **René Dorand** set helicopter altitude and speed records in 1936. The following year, Germany's Focke-Achgelis Company built a machine with two

Igor Sikorsky piloting his helicopter

rotors side by side, and it broke both French records.

Sikorsky, however, came up with a better design. His idea was to place a small vertical rotor at the end of a long tail to counteract the torque of the top-mounted lifting rotor. He successfully flew the **VS-300** prototype in September 1939. It was an important breakthrough that set the course for all future helicopter development. The VS-300 was the world's first successful rotary-winged vehicle, and its configuration remains the most common to this day. Sikorsky did not invent the helicopter, but he made it feasible. The production model, the VS-300A, was ready in 1941, but saw only limited action in World War II. The helicopter first began to prove its military usefulness in 1950 during the Korean War.

No More Runs

The armed forces found immediate uses for a new material introduced in

1939 at the World's Fair in New York. Developed by **Wallace H. Carothers** and his research team at the Du Pont Company, **nylon** was the first purely artificial fiber. Produced entirely from chemicals, it is best known for its use in stockings, but after the U.S. entered World War II all nylon production was aimed at providing equipment such as parachutes, tents, mosquito nets, and surgical thread for the war effort.

Before nylon, stockings were primarily made of silk, an expensive and delicate natural fiber. To come up with an inexpensive synthetic alternative, Du Pont hired Carothers, an organic chemist at Harvard University, in 1928 to lead the research at the firm's Delaware laboratory.

Du Pont believed the answer lay in **polymerization**, the process of chemically combining molecules of the same compound into long chains of larger molecules called polymers. With recent advances in organic chemistry, Du Pont realized that it might be possible to turn basic chemicals into polymers like the ones found in nature, such as silk. These chemicals, called **hydrocarbons**, were readily available as byproducts of the growing oil-refining industry. Because the physical characteristics of materials depend on their molecular structure, it would also be possible to customize these substances to have predetermined characteristics.

In 1907, Leo Baekeland had created

the first synthetic polymer when he invented Bakelite and launched the plastics industry, but no one knew what held these molecules together. In 1930 Carothers concluded that polymers were held together the same way as other molecules; the only difference was their extreme length.

That same year, Carothers created a synthetic rubber called **Neoprene** from polymers. Neoprene became vital to the Allied forces during World War II after the Japanese occupied and controlled Malaya, the world's main source of natural rubber.

Carothers and his team concocted a new substance in 1934, with a similar molecular structure to silk, but it was much weaker than the natural material, and its melting point was too high to be spun into fibers. After further tinkering, the team discovered that the substance could stick to the tip of a glass stirring rod and stretch out all the way down the lab's hall in a fine strand. This drawn-out filament was the artificial silk substitute they were hoping to discover.

By 1935, Carothers had been using a process called **"cold drawing"** to create these long threads. By melting the polymers and squeezing them through tiny holes, cold drawing aligned the molecules to produce lightweight fibers found to be stronger than silk.

Although televi000sion made its public American debut at the 1939 World's Fair, nylon stole the show.

Dr. Wallace Corothers in his lab

"Nylon can be fashioned into filaments as strong as steel, as fine as a spider's web, yet more elastic than any of the common natural fibers," Du Pont vice president Charles Stine told the astonished crowd.

Sadly, the chronically depressed Carothers did not live to see the success of his creation. He killed himself with a dose of cyanide on April 29, 1937, only three weeks after the patent for nylon was filed and two days after his 41st birthday.

Du Pont sold 60 million pairs of nylon stockings (or simply "nylons," as they came to be called) by 1941. Today, the versatile fabric is also used for items such as rope, toothbrushes, sails, clothing, strings for musical instruments, and shoelaces. Nylon does not shrink and is resistant to grease, dirt, and mildew, as well as moths and other destructive insects.

TEFLON

A result of unrelated research at the Du Pont laboratories, Teflon is best known as the non-stick coating used in cookware. In 1938 Roy J. Plunkett was working on developing a non-toxic refrigerant when he examined a cylinder he expected to be filled with gas; instead, it contained a slippery white powder. The gas had polymerized into a long chain of molecules and solidified into the most slippery substance in the world.

"But that's the thing about a discovery," Plunkett later said. "Even though (the experiment) did go wrong, you go ahead and find out what you got."

Because Teflon is extremely non-corrosive, the U.S. Army used it during World War II in the world's first atomic bombs. Du Pont secretly manufactured the substance for this purpose, and it was only after the war that the public learned of Teflon's existence. Teflon is resistant to acids, bases, heat, and solvents; because it is highly inert, the body does not reject it, making Teflon an ideal material for artificial limbs and heart valves. NASA has also extensively used Teflon for space missions.

The Bug That Wouldn't Die

Versatility was also one of the main reasons for the success of the **Volkswagen Beetle**. Powered by a unique air-cooled engine, the German car proved its reliability during World War II, running in the harsh Russian winter as well as in the boiling-hot Sahara Desert.

Shortly after Hitler became chancellor of Germany in 1933, he commissioned automotive engineer **Ferdinand Porsche** to produce a car every German could afford — a Volkswagen, or people's car. After Porsche submitted a design the following year, Hitler approved the construction of a new factory in Wolfsburg to manufacture Volkswagens.

But there was a catch: The car had to sell for no more than 1,000 German Reichsmarks, a price more in the range of motorcycles. This was no easy task, but one of Porsche's engineers, **Franz Reimspeiss**, designed an inexpensive four-cylinder engine to be placed in the rear of the car, and soon the Wolfsburg automobile plant, the world's largest, was in business. The war soon began, and the military versions of the Beetle served the Germans well. Despite heavy damage from Allied bombers, the Volkswagen plant never stopped churning out cars. After the war, new management took over and, no longer limited by Hitler's price restrictions, began to use higher-quality materials.

The Beetle, or Bug, made its American debut in 1949. The philosophy behind the Volkswagen was in many ways similar to that of Ford's Model T. Both were extremely successful, and in 1972 the Beetle replaced the Model T as the most numerously produced car in history. Volkswagen had made more than 19 million Bugs by the time its German plant discontinued the model in 1978. This, however, was not the end of its production run; factories in Mexico and Brazil still make the tough little car, based on the same basic design of 1934.

Modernizing the Office

Another brilliant idea originated in 1934 when American **Chester F. Carlson** began working on a machine that could produce fast and inexpensive reproductions of documents. A graduate of the California Institute of Technology, Carlson knew he wanted to be an inventor, but the depressed economy forced him to take a job in the patents department of a New York electronics company. One of his duties was to produce copies of documents and drawings, and the only way to do it was by hand. This was a very tedious process, and he decided to find a better way.

Carlson first looked into photography, but decided that photographic developing was too long and messy a procedure for an office environment. Then he turned to **selenium**, the photoelectric cell that made electronic television possible. He used a mirror to project the image of the document onto a drum coated with electrically charged selenium. The more light that hit a particular point on the drum, the more the charges were dispersed. When negatively charged powder was released onto the drum, it adhered to the positively charged dark areas. The final step was to use heat to transfer the powder onto a positively charged sheet of paper.

Chester Carlson

It took four years to make the machine work, but Carlson finally produced the world's first dry copy of the handwritten text, "10-22-38 Astoria," referring to the date and location (Astoria is in Queens, New York) of the successful experiment. He called the process **"xerography"**, derived from the Greek, meaning "dry writing."

Carlson soon discovered, however, that technical success did not translate into immediate financial success. After shopping his machine around, he could not find a company that was interested in his invention; they all insisted the market was too small. Carlson finally convinced a small company, the Haloid Company, to take a chance.

The first copier, the Xerox Model A, went on sale in 1949. The large and complicated machine, nicknamed the **"ox box"**, was a commercial flop. It was only in 1960, when a later model using toner was introduced, allowing it to be used with ordinary paper, that Carlson's

The Carlson copier

computers, which perform operations using only numbers, Bush's machine was an analog computer, or one that makes computations by taking physical measurements — much like a bathroom scale or a thermostat. An improved version was completed in 1935; the 100-ton analyzer had 150 motors and 100 miles of wire connecting a seemingly endless array of vacuum tubes, gears, axles, and rotating rods. Programming the computer was a laborious process involving screwdrivers and hammers, but once the settings were in order the differential analyzer could solve equations, with up to 18 variables, 100 times faster than a human using a calculator today.

The differential analyzer would eventually give way to more advanced computers that would become smaller, faster, and increasingly prominent in daily life. In the 1930s, however, few people knew what a computer was, and not many more knew about television and radar. Yet these technologies would play a vital role in shaping our world in the ensuing decades.

machine began making money. The Haloid Company became the Xerox Corporation in 1961, and Carlson became a multimillionaire from royalty payments and company stock.

Like photocopiers, computers are now standard equipment in most offices. The predecessor of the modern computer was the **differential analyzer** built by Professor **Vannevar Bush** of the Massachusetts Institute of Technology in 1930. Unlike today's digital

TECHNOLOGY

chapter 5

1940-1949

Another World War Spawns the Nuclear Age

Mushroom cloud over Nagasaki, Japan

The 1940s marked an important turning point in human history. The decade began in the midst of the largest and deadliest war the world has ever experienced, and along the way humankind discovered how to destroy the planet by harnessing the power of the basic building blocks of matter. The atomic bomb opened the door to an age in which the threat of war also meant the possibility of world destruction. Few mythological deities ever possessed such awesome power.

Even before nuclear weapons threatened every person on the planet, war was no longer just for soldiers; extensive aerial bombings of major cities in World War II killed millions of civilians, and Hitler's concentration camps systematically exterminated millions more.

Germany had begun the war with resounding success. After easily conquering Denmark, Norway, the Netherlands, and Belgium, Hitler attacked France. To prevent another German attack as in World War I, France had poured much of its resources into building a defensive barrier called the Maginot Line along its border with Germany. This was a different kind of war, however. Striking from Belgium, Hitler's highly mobile army simply went around the stationary fortifications, defeated the mighty French army, and took control of France within a month — something Germany could not do in the entire four years of World War I. The Germans set up a puppet regime in France called the Vichy government, but rebellious citizens formed the French resistance to fight back against their conquerors.

With much of Europe under Axis control, Great Britain became the only major power standing against the aggressors. Hitler's air force, the Luftwaffe,

LONG-PLAYING RECORD

In November 1931 RCA Victor released the first long-playing (LP) record with a recording of Beethoven's Fifth Symphony. The 12-inch disk was the same size as previous records, but it was designed to spin at a rate of 33 1/3 revolutions per minute (rpm), an improvement over its 78 rpm predecessor. In addition to its slower speed, the LP had grooves of smaller width, called "microgrooves," which allowed for more than twice as many grooves per inch. This allowed LPs to hold about 23 minutes of music on each side, while 78 rpm records were limited to six minutes per side. The poor economy of the Great Depression, however, did not allow the new records to gain a foothold in the marketplace. In 1948 Columbia Records introduced an improved LP developed by engineers Peter Goldmark and William Bachman. Pressed on vinyl, the new LPs were more durable and less noisy than older records made of shellac. This time the LP revolutionized the industry and the 78 rpm record quickly became obsolete. Also using microgrooves pressed on vinyl, RCA introduced the 7-inch, 45 rpm format in 1949. The shorter duration established it as the standard format for "singles," releases featuring one song on each side.

began bombing England in July 1940 in an attempt to destroy the Royal Air Force (RAF) and crush British morale in preparation for a full-scale German invasion, dubbed Operation Sea Lion. Using Britain's newly developed radar system, the heavily outnumbered RAF successfully defended their homeland against the Germans. The defeat forced Hitler to cancel Operation Sea Lion in October and turn east.

After extending his empire into Hungary, Romania, Bulgaria, Yugoslavia, and Greece, Hitler reneged on his non-aggression pact with Stalin and attacked the Soviet Union in June 1941. The Germans got as close as 20 miles to Moscow, but the combination of the harsh Russian winter and a Soviet counterattack forced Hitler's army to retreat for the first time. Meanwhile, in North Africa, German Field Marshal Erwin Rommel's tank divisions took Libya from the British.

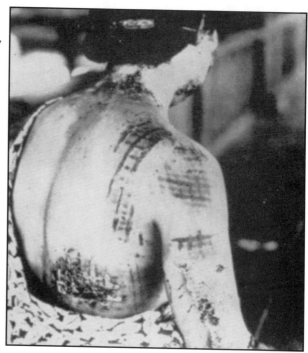

Atom bomb victim, 1944

The Japanese navy attacked the American Pacific Fleet at Pearl Harbor, Hawaii, on December 7, 1941, and the U.S. immediately entered the war in the Pacific and Europe. It was now truly a world war.

During World War II the aircraft carrier become the most important vessel in naval combat. When the Americans defeated the Japanese in the Battle of the Coral Sea in 1942, it was the world's first naval battle fought entirely by carrier-based aircraft. The Battle of Midway the following month was another such battle. This was Japan's last offensive and a major turning point in the Pacific war. Launching a counteroffensive, the U.S. landed its troops on Guadalcanal in the Solomon Islands in August and began slow process of island-hopping toward the Japanese homeland.

In 1943 the German Sixth Army finally surrendered to the Soviets at Stalingrad after one of the deadliest battles in history. With the U.S. in the war, the Allies drove the Axis forces out of North Africa and set their sights on Europe. After taking the island of Sicily, the Allies landed in southern Italy and began their slow drive up the boot-shaped peninsula.

> **"I feel about it much as I do about fire. I regret its damage, but I am glad the human race discovered it."**
>
> Orville Wright, after being asked during WWII if he was sorry for inventing the airplane.

The tide had turned for the Axis powers. By the middle of 1944 the U.S.S.R. had driven Germany from most of its territory, and on June 6 the Allies launched the D-Day invasion of France's Normandy coast, the largest amphibious invasion in history. The Allies had liberated France by the end of August, and began to head toward Germany's capital city of Berlin.

Along the way, British troops liberated the concentration camp at Bergen-Belsen, and the world learned of the Holocaust and the extent of Hitler's atrocities. His "final solution to the Jewish problem" was to exterminate them all. Six million people, mostly Jews, perished in the death camps. Most died in the gas chambers, but others were subjected to horrific experiments conducted by the Nazis.

By February 1945 the outcome of the war was fairly obvious, and the leaders of the three main Allied powers — Winston Churchill of Great Britain, Franklin Delano Roosevelt of the United States, and Joseph Stalin of the U.S.S.R. — met at Yalta in the Soviet Union to decide what to do with Germany after its impending defeat. They decided to divide the country and Berlin into four zones, three of which would be controlled by the three nations, and the fourth by France.

The Soviets reached Berlin first on April 20, and Hitler committed suicide 10 days later. Germany unconditionally surrendered on May 8, as millions celebrated V-E (Victory in Europe) Day. In an effort to prevent future wars, the Allies formed a world organization called the United Nations (U.N.) to settle international disputes peacefully. Most nations in the world would eventually become members of the U.N.

The war was not yet over in the Pacific, however. Although Allied troops had landed on the Japanese island of Okinawa in April and strategic bombing had destroyed nearly half of Tokyo by July, the Japanese refused to surrender. Only after the United States dropped atomic bombs on the cities of Hiroshima and Nagasaki in August did Japan capitulate. On September 2, 1945 — six years, one day, and 55 million deaths after Hitler's invasion of Poland started World War II — Japan signed the formal surrender that officially ended the war.

The balance of power had greatly changed after the war. For centuries Western European nations had been the dominant world powers, but by war's end the U.S. and the U.S.S.R. took over these roles. Because the two nations, operating under contrasting political and economic systems, had different and often conflicting goals and agendas, a long period of international tension called the "Cold War" emerged. In response to the Soviet Union's forcefully spreading its sphere of communist influence throughout Eastern Europe shortly after the war, U.S. President Harry S. Truman issued the Truman Doctrine, a pledge to help nations around the world defend themselves against communism.

In 1949 the United States, Great Britain, and France consolidated their zones in Germany into a democratic nation, the Federal Republic of Germany, also known as West Germany. The U.S.S.R. turned its zone into a communist state, the German Democratic Republic, or East Germany.

Communism also spread eastward after the war. Formerly a Japanese colony, Korea gained independence in 1948, and the following year it was divided at the 38th parallel into two nations. The United States established the Republic of Korea south of the line, and the Soviet Union created the Democratic People's Republic of Korea in the north. Mao Zedong finally won the power struggle for control of China in 1949. He instituted a communist government and changed the nation's name to the People's Republic of China. The defeated Chiang Kai-shek fled to Taiwan (Formosa) and formed the Republic of China, an independent state.

The "Fat Man" bomb

The Cold War quickly spread all over the world, and tensions further increased after the U.S.S.R. developed its own atomic bomb in 1949. That same year, the U.S. and Western European nations joined forces and formed the North Atlantic Treaty Organization (NATO) to oppose the perceived Soviet threat. The existence of nuclear weapons changed the way governments handled international relations. The consequences of another world war had the potential to be more grave than those of any previous conflict.

Like most wars, World War II triggered rapid technological advances. Aviation entered a new era with the development of the jet engine, and rockets designed by German scientists became the foundation for future space exploration. The end of the war allowed technology to focus once again on developing less destructive and even constructive innovations. The invention of the transistor opened the door to a new world of electronic possibilities, which triggered the rapid progress in computer development characteristic of

the second half of the century. Still, in the years after the war, the world had to learn to live with the possibility of nuclear warfare annihilating the planet.

Power Redefined

By the time World War II had started in 1939, the world's scientific community was well aware of the enormous amounts of energy that could potentially be unleashed from an atomic nucleus. Much of the basis for atomic energy theory came from German physicist **Albert Einstein's Special Theory of Relativity**. Published in 1905, the theory included the famous equation $E = mc^2$, which states that the energy in any particle of matter is equal to its mass multiplied by the square of the speed of light (186,000 miles per second). By this reasoning, even the smallest amount of matter is capable of releasing immense quantities of energy.

In 1934 Hungarian physicist **Leo Szilard**, who had come to London to

Enrico Fermi

tute for Chemistry. **Uranium**, the heaviest naturally occurring element, especially intrigued them, but Meitner could not continue her work under Nazi rule because she was Jewish. She escaped Germany in 1938, and settled in Sweden. Hahn continued the research without her, but the two scientists continued to collaborate through the mail. A few months later Hahn had a major breakthrough: He split the uranium atom and created a new element, a **radioactive** form of the metal **barium**. When Meitner received word of the development, she and her nephew, physicist Otto Frisch, mathematically calculated that splitting the uranium atom created a relatively huge amount of energy. They called the process **"fission"**, a term used in chemistry to describe the way bacteria multiply by splitting in two.

Scientists soon realized that one or more neutrons from a split nucleus could be used to split other uranium nuclei and create a chain reaction like the one Szilard envisioned in 1934. By 1939, it was estimated that nuclear fission could harness enough energy from one ounce of uranium to produce an explosion equivalent in force to 600 tons of the explosive TNT (trimitrotoluene). The possibility of Nazi Germany's developing a weapon utilizing these principles terrified Szilard, Einstein, and other renowned scientists. In a letter dated August 2, 1939, they notified President Roosevelt of the situation. On December 6, 1941, the day before the Japanese attack on Pearl Harbor and America's entry into the war, Roosevelt officially initiated the American development of atomic weapons. To keep the project secret, its name was unrelated to

escape the Nazi regime in 1933, came up with a theory for an atomic bomb. He reasoned that if an element was found that could be split by a neutron (a subatomic particle with no electric charge), a nuclear chain reaction could be initiated. The energy from such a reaction could then be unleashed by an atomic bomb. Szilard didn't know which element would be appropriate for these purposes and lacked the funds to conduct the necessary research, so he patented his idea and gave it to the British government to protect it as an official secret.

In Berlin, German chemist **Otto Hahn** and Austrian physicist **Lise Meitner** had been bombarding various chemical elements with neutrons in the late 1930s at the Kaiser Wilhelm Insti-

the purpose: the **Manhattan Engineering District**, more commonly known as the **Manhattan Project**.

Roosevelt appointed Nobel Prize-winning physicist **Enrico Fermi** to lead the research and construction of a practical nuclear reactor. Fermi and his Jewish wife had fled the anti-Semitism of fascist Italy in 1938 and settled in Chicago.

In November 1942 Fermi and his team began assembling the world's first nuclear reactor in a squash court underneath an abandoned football stadium on the **University of Chicago** campus. A chain reaction caused by nuclear fission could theoretically produce a constant flow of energy, but the problem was keeping it under control, for the chain reaction could overheat and cause a nuclear explosion.

Fermi's earlier Nobel Prize-winning work showed that slowing down the bombarding neutrons increased the probability of producing a reaction. Fermi chose to use blocks of graphite, a form of pure carbon, intermingled with the uranium to slow down the neutrons. The reactor was called a **pile** because the materials were piled on top of each other. Ten rods made of the metal cadmium were placed in the 25-foot-wide pile to absorb the neutrons and keep the reactor under control during construction. There could be no reaction as long as the cadmium rods were in place.

On December 2, 1942, the pile was complete, and Fermi ordered the careful removal of the cadmium control rods. It was a tense moment, for if there were faults in his design the reactor could explode and destroy most of Chicago. There was no explosion, however, and Fermi had succeeded in creating the first manmade, self-sustaining nuclear chain reaction. Using a predetermined code,

Robert Oppenheimer and General Leslie Groves at ground zero

the team notified government officials by telegram. "The Italian navigator has just landed in the New World," the wire read.

The nuclear reaction also produced a new element, **plutonium**, not found in nature, and the scientists reasoned it could also be used to create such reactions. Newly constructed plants in Oak Ridge, Tennessee, and Hanford, Washington, soon began producing both uranium and plutonium. An elaborate laboratory was built in **Los Alamos**, New Mexico, where scientists and engineers conducted further research on uranium, plutonium, and bomb design. The Army appointed American physicist **J. Robert** **Oppenheimer** as scientific director of the Manhattan Project.

By 1945 the Oak Ridge and Hanford plants had produced enough uranium for one bomb and enough plutonium for two. The plutonium device was a more difficult design, and there was some doubt about whether it would work, so a test, known as the **Trinity** test, was arranged. In the desert near Alamagordo, New Mexico, about 200 miles from Los Alamos, the bomb was placed atop a 100-foot steel tower to reduce the amount of sand sucked up by the blast, which would then fall to the earth as radioactive debris. On July 12 the world's first nuclear bomb exploded with the power equivalent to 20,000 tons of TNT.

"Suddenly, there was an enormous flash of light," Polish-born physicist Isidor I. Rabi said, describing the blast. "It bored its way right through you. It was a vision which was seen with more than just the eye...There was an enormous ball of fire which grew and grew and it rolled as it grew; it went up into the air, in yellow flashes and into scarlet and green. It seemed to come toward one."

The world had entered the nuclear age, and Rabi realized the significance of such a development. "A new thing had just been born," he said. "A new control; a new understanding of man, which man had acquired over nature."

On August 6, 1945, an American Boeing B-29 bomber named the **Enola Gay** flew over the Japanese city of **Hiroshima** and dropped the untested uranium bomb, nicknamed **Little Boy** because it was smaller than its plutonium counterpart.

"Where before there had been a city with distinctive houses, buildings and everything that you could see from our

SILLY PUTTY

Perhaps the strangest and most entertaining product to come out of World War II was Silly Putty. Trying to concoct an artificial substitute for rubber, General Electric engineer James Wright combined boric acid with silicone oil in 1943. The result was a gooey, bouncy blob. It soon became obvious that the substance was not suitable for making tires, but Wright was intrigued by it. He consulted his colleagues, but no one could think of a practical use for it. The only thing they knew for sure was that the stuff was fun to play with. Before long, news of the bouncy goo spread throughout the scientific and engineering world. In 1949, advertising copywriter Peter Hodgson heard about it and figured out what the scientists could not: how to use the putty to make money. Hodgson borrowed $147 and bought a large batch from General Electric. He cut the goo up into one-ounce globs, put each into a small plastic egg, and named it Silly Putty. Priced at $1, it made its debut at Doubleday bookshops in New York and soon became a huge success. Silly Putty became so popular that in 1968 Apollo 8 astronauts brought some along with them for the first manned orbit of the moon. But that is another chapter in the story of technology.

altitude," Colonel Paul Tibbets, pilot of the Enola Gay, said of the bombing's immediate aftermath, "now you couldn't see anything except a black boiling debris down below."

The blast killed 80,000 people and destroyed the city. Three days later, **Fat Man**, the plutonium bomb, killed 40,000 people in **Nagasaki**. Japan surrendered the next day, unaware that the U.S. had no more atomic bombs at its immediate disposal.

After the end of World War II, the U.S. emerged as the leading world power and the only nation with nuclear weapon technology, but this situation did not last long. The U.S.S.R. detonated its first atomic bomb in 1949, and a nuclear arms race followed between the rival nations for the next 40 years.

Propellerless Propulsion

The decade's most important advance in aviation was the **jet engine**, and like the atomic bomb, it was used in battle only after the war's outcome had been decided.

By the time World War II broke out in 1939, propeller-powered monoplanes had replaced biplanes as the preferred aircraft design. Planes flew faster, higher, and farther than those of World War I. Most were made of steel with enclosed cockpits, and could carry heavier payloads, which meant more weapons such as bombs or machine guns. Radio communication had also become an integral part of aviation. Despite all these advances, airplanes still were propelled using the same principles used by the Wright brothers in 1903. A radically different propulsion system was already in the works well before World War II began.

The limitations of the propeller-driven system were beginning to be felt. Airplanes were flying as fast as propellers could take them, and propellers, it was discovered, operated less efficiently at high altitudes, where the air is thinner.

British RAF pilot and engineer **Frank Whittle** thought he had the solution to these problems. In 1930 he patented a design for a jet engine, which mixes fuel with the oxygen in the surrounding air, ignites the mixture in its combustion chamber, and produces a high-speed exhaust that propels the vehicle forward. The jet engine produced much more power relative to its weight than a propeller driven by an internal combustion engine. The British Air Ministry, however, was not yet interested in Whittle's new design.

Like so many other innovations throughout the history of technology, two people working independently of each other developed similar breakthroughs at around the same time. In Germany, aeronautical engineer **Hans von Ohain** patented a similar design for a jet engine in 1935, and began developing it the following year for aircraft manufacturer **Ernst Heinkel**. On August 27, 1939, just a few days before Hitler started the war, a **Heinkel He 178** became the world's first jet-propelled aircraft to fly. "The hideous wail of the engine was music to our ears," Heinkel said.

By this time, Whittle had gained the British government's support and was developing his engine. In May 1941 it finally made its first flight in an experimental Gloster E28/39 airplane.

"Frank, it flies," exclaimed a spectator at the test flight, and Whittle replied, "That was what it was bloody well designed to do, wasn't it?"

MICROWAVE OVEN

Radar not only helped save Britain from the invading Germans, but also led to the invention of the microwave oven and for the first time in history allowed humans to cook food without fire. One day in 1946, engineer Percy L. Spencer of the Raytheon Company in Massachusetts stood in front of a magnetron, the microwave generator used in radar detection, and noticed that the candy bar in his pocket had melted. After investigating the incident, he discovered that microwave radiation can cook food by causing molecules to vibrate rapidly and generate heat. The discovery was timely for Raytheon, since World War II had recently ended and the military no longer needed so many magnetrons for radar-detection equipment. Raytheon applied the technology to microwave ovens and released the first model, the Radarange, in 1947. The five-foot-tall, 750-pound ovens sold for $3,000 each and were used primarily on trains and ships and in restaurants. Microwave ovens did not become popular for domestic use until Raytheon's newly acquired subsidiary Amana Refrigeration released a compact and affordable model in 1967 priced at $495.

When Germany's **Messerschmitt Me 262**, powered by two of von Ohain's engines, flew in 1942, it became the world's first jet fighter and had a top speed of 540 miles an hour. The British

Gloster Meteor, with a top speed of 480 miles an hour, followed in 1943. After some modifications, the Meteor became the first jet fighter to enter military service the next year. The faster and superior German Me 262 flew into battle in 1944, and was the first jet fighter to engage an enemy plane. More Me 262s were produced during the war than any other jet fighter, but it was too late to help Hitler's cause.

Germany also developed the **V-1** flying bomb, also called the **"buzz bomb"** or "Doodlebug," which was basically a pilotless and explosive jet-propelled aircraft. The "V" stood for Vergeltungswaffen, or vengeance weapon, because these missiles were intended to repay the British for their bombing raids on Berlin. Hitler began attacking London with V-1s in 1944. A buzz bomb would fly toward its target, and once it reached its preset range the engine would stop, putting the V-1 into a deadly dive. Germany launched more than 8,000 V-1s against the British during the war, but because they flew at the relatively low speed of 450 miles per hour, V-1s were vulnerable to fighter planes. On several occasions, British fighter pilots actually knocked Doodlebugs off their designated courses by softly nudging them with their planes' wings.

Using Whittle's jet-engine design, the American aircraft company Lockheed developed the F-80 Shooting Star jet fighter in 1943. Initially plagued with problems, the Shooting Star was significantly improved by 1947, and set the world speed record of 623 miles per hour.

This record didn't last long. Fighter planes during the war could almost approach the speed of sound in a dive, but the planes would become difficult to control at that speed. After the war, aviators began wondering weather supersonic flight was possible. It was known that at their fastest, air molecules move at the speed of sound, or **Mach 1**, and move out of the way of slower-flying objects. If a plane traveled faster, a common theory stated, the molecules would pile up in front, and the aircraft would be flying into a **"sound barrier"** of compressed air, which was likened to flying into a wall. The flaw with this theory was obvious, by the fact that that there were already objects that moved faster than sound, such as bullets, artillery shells, and the tip of a bullwhip.

On October 14, 1947, U.S. Air Force Captain **Chuck Yeager** ended the speculation. He flew the **Bell X-1** research craft faster than anyone had ever traveled, and broke the sound barrier. The bullet-shaped plane was powered by a rocket engine, which, unlike a jet engine, used liquid oxygen rather than the oxygen in the surrounding air. Launched from an airborne B-29 bomber at 12,000 feet to conserve fuel, the X-1 gained alti-

tude and encountered turbulent shock waves as it approached Mach 0.96. Yeager finally broke the sound barrier at 43,000 feet and reached a speed of Mach 1.04 (700 miles an hour). At this speed, the turbulence stopped, and the aircraft became easier to control.

Spectators on the ground heard a loud noise called a **sonic boom**. As it turns out, the compressed air in front of an object traveling at the speed of sound does not act like a wall; rather, it slips to the side and expands again, causing a sonic boom. The sound made by the crack of a whip is actually a smaller version of this phenomenon.

> **"The thing I deplore most is the use of solid-state electronics by rock-and-roll musicians to raise the level of sound to where it is both painful and injurous."**
>
> Walter H. Brattain, co-inventor of the transistor, 1973

V-2 Vengeance weapon

1946 ENIAC computer

first ballistic missile. Later renamed the **V-2**, or **vengeance weapon number two**, it was repeatedly launched against London like its predecessor, the V-1. Flying at supersonic speeds, the 46-foot-tall rocket was impossible to catch by any existing aircraft. Its victims had no hopes of defense, but as was the case with Germany's jet fighters, the V-2 came too late to turn the war around for Hitler.

As the war was ending, Hitler ordered all his rocket experts, including von Braun, killed to prevent the Allies from capturing them and utilizing their expertise. The team managed to evade their would-be executioners as Berlin was falling, and surrendered to the American forces. Just as Hitler had feared, the German engineers went to work for the Allied countries. In 1946 von Braun and his colleagues launched the first of several captured V-2 rockets at White Sands in New Mexico. The German scientists and engineers would play a vital role in the future success of the U.S. space program.

Rocket technology was also used during World War II. Despite his successes with rockets, Robert Goddard's work did not interest the U.S. military until after the war, by which time Goddard had died. Germany, on the other hand, was very interested in rockets. The German army realized that the Treaty of Versailles did not limit the production of rockets, and in 1933 it appointed **Wernher von Braun** to lead the research.

Von Braun had fallen in love with rocketry at an early age, but contrary to Hitler's agenda, he was more interested in its potential as a vehicle for space exploration than as a destructive weapon. The Nazi regime forbade any rocket research that did not serve its military needs, and once even arrested von Braun for allegedly studying space flight. Because he was so valuable to the war effort, he was held for only two weeks.

By 1942 von Braun and his team had developed the A4 rocket, the world's

Smaller Is Better

World War II also inspired advances in computer technology. In Great Britain, a secret project led by mathematician **Alan M. Turing** developed a series of computers to decipher messages sent by Germany's **Enigma coding** machines. The first of these machines was called **The Bombe**, and it worked well until the Germans improved their Enigma system. The British also improved their equipment, and in 1943 a much improved machine was ready for use. The aptly named **Colossus** filled a large room and used 1,500 vacuum tubes to effectively break the German code. An improved version with 2,400 valves, the **Mark II Colossus**, began service the following year. These huge computers generated so much heat that the operators had to work with their shirts off. This project was top secret, and the machines were destroyed after the war; thus, little is known about them to this day.

Across the Atlantic, two instructors at the University of Pennsylvania's Moore School of Electrical Engineering, **John Mauchly** and **John P. Eckert**, began work on a computer for the U.S. Army to calculate artillery trajectory tables. The result was another giant called **ENIAC**, the Electronic Numerical Integrator and Computer. Completed in 1946, the 30-ton machine was 100 feet long, 10 feet high, three feet deep, and contained 18,000 vacuum tubes connected by 500 miles of wire.

At the time, ENIAC was the fastest computer in the world, but it had its problems. Even with its own air conditioner, ENIAC had trouble staying cool and normally ran for only an hour at a time. The heat also attracted moths, which were often electrocuted by the high-voltage machine.

Short circuits usually followed, and ENIAC became the first computer to be **"debugged."** If one of its many vacuum tubes faltered, finding the faulty valve could take up to eight hours. Perhaps its most significant drawback was the long process required to set the machine up for different functions, or programs. The necessary switching, replugging, and rearranging often took days to complete.

Although Colossus and ENIAC were a big step forward, their reliance on so many vacuum tubes was a limitation to further computer advances. These valves, a basic component in electrical equipment from radios to telephone switching systems as well as early computers, served two main purposes: increasing electrical current (**amplification**) and forcing the current in one direction (**rectification**). Vacuum tubes were bulky, fragile, expensive, and power-hungry, and they often overheated.

(l. to r.) **Drs. John Bardeen, William Shockley and Walter Brattan at Bell Labs, 1948**

In 1945 Bell Telephone Laboratories assembled a team of researchers to see if they could come up with a **"solid state"** substitute for the vacuum tube. A solid-state device is one which, as its name implies, is solid and has no moving parts, unlike a thermionic valve, which operates in the vacuum of a glass bulb. **William Shockley, John Bardeen,** and **Walter Brattain** headed the research. They decided to focus on **semiconductors,** chemically treated crystals of silicon or germanium that conduct or resist current. Most materials are either conductors, such as metals, or insulators, such as plastic, but semiconductors could act as both. Until that time, semiconductors had been used as rectifiers, but no one had figured out how to make them work as amplifiers.

Success came in December 1947, when the team amplified a signal using germanium crystals in a new invention called the transfer resistor, or **transistor.** Placed between two areas of semiconductor crystals, a transistor could perform the functions of a vacuum tube — faster while using a very small current and generating little heat in a compact size. Transistors were relatively easy and inexpensive to manufacture, and because they were solid, they were very durable, unlike fragile vacuum tubes, whose heating filaments had a limited life span. The breakthrough would soon revolutionize electronics by making products cheaper, smaller, more reliable, and more versatile while opening the door to future innovations that would continue this trend.

Products of War

In a decade remembered primarily for World War II, most of the weapons used were improvements or modifications of previously existing devices, such as airplanes, tanks, and submarines, which first saw significant military action in World War I.

The adaptation of the airplane to ship-based operation was a major development of World War II. Pioneered by

1946 Vacuum Tube Systems

the U.S., Great Britain, and Japan in the 1920s, the first **aircraft carriers**, or flattops, were converted battle cruisers. By World War II, aircraft carriers, each capable of carrying up to 100 aircraft and 3,500 personnel, were sophisticated vessels with flight decks, hangars, and support services for aircraft.

> **"Is it progress if a cannibal uses a fork?"**
>
> Stanislaw J. Lec, Unkempt Thoughts

Beginning with the Japanese carrier fleet's attack on Pearl Harbor in 1941, aircraft carriers dominated military operations in the war's Pacific Theater. The **Battle of the Coral Sea** in 1942 was the first naval battle in which the opposing fleets were not even in sight of each other. Armed with bombs, torpedoes, and machine guns, aircraft were the only offensive weapons used in the war's first great American victory over Japan. The following month, Japanese and American fleets clashed at the **Battle of Midway**, resulting in U.S. planes sinking or severely damaging all four of the Japanese fleet's aircraft carriers. After this defeat, Japan began fighting a defensive war as American forces slowly worked their way closer to the Japanese homeland.

On land, the **tank** became a vital weapon. To counter its effectiveness, anti-tank weapons were introduced. The most famous of these was the American rocket launcher, nicknamed the **"bazooka"** because the tube-like weapon resembled a musical instrument used by American comedian Bob Burns. Developed in 1941, the bazooka fired a 2.36-inch-diameter rocket from an infantryman's shoulder. Its light weight allowed one person to easily carry it,

and the 21-inch-long rocket, traveling at 265 feet per second, could penetrate five inches of armor. Bazookas first appeared on the battlefield in 1942. The Germans soon captured a bazooka and by the end of the year had developed their own version called the Panzerschreck (tank terror).

Also in 1942, scientists at Harvard University developed an incendiary substance called **napalm**, a mixture of gasoline and other fuels with a gelling agent. Napalm stuck to anything it touched and burned with intense heat. Although originally intended as an efficient fuel for flame throwers, it was also used as filler for bombs. The U.S. first used napalm in its aerial bombing of Japanese industrial targets on Guadalcanal.

> **"Progress imposes not only new possibilities for the future but new restrictions."**
>
> Norbert Weiner, The Human Use of Human Beings

One of the most innovative bombs of World War II was the bouncing bomb developed by British aeronautical engineer Barnes Wallis. Also called the skipping bomb, its purpose was to destroy German dams. The bomb hung diagonally in the bay of a bomber, and just before the drop an electric motor spun it backwards. This made the bomb skip across the water surface until it hit the dam, but instead of detonating on impact, it first submerged about 30 feet under the water and then exploded, maximizing the damage inflicted on the target. By destroying dams, bouncing bombs helped cut off German industries from their power sources.

Also hoping to inflict damage in the

water, French naval officer **Jacques-Yves Cousteau** invented the aqualung. An experienced diver, Cousteau was a member of the Resistance during Germany's occupation of France and realized that a Self-Contained Underwater Breathing Apparatus (also known as **SCUBA**) would be valuable in sabotaging German ships. Although various contraptions had been used over the centuries to allow man to explore the sea, none allowed divers to swim underwater without a connection to the surface. Pressurized-air canisters already existed, but the main problem was regulating the appropriate air pressure relative to the water's depth. The air supply's pressure needed to be increased as the diver descended, so that the air would enter the lungs.

In 1942 Cousteau met with French engineer **Emile Gagnan**, who had invented a pressure-reducing demand valve that enabled cars to run on propane during the war's gasoline shortage. The two men adapted this valve to deliver air from a pressurized cylinder at the correct pressure for the diver. The result was the aqualung, or scuba. After the war, Cousteau became world-famous for his underwater films of marine life, which were made possible by his invention.

Once the war ended, the world braced itself for the atomic age. Life in the postwar world would see significant change. With the arrival of the jet engine and the transistor, humankind made great strides in transportation and electronics, but of all the developments to come out of the 1940s, the legacy of the atomic bomb would be the most profound. The world was not only shrinking, it was becoming more delicate.

Jacques Cousteau

TECHNOLOGY

chapter 6

1950-1959

Shooting for the Stars

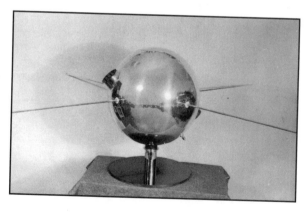

1959 Vanguard II, first weather satellite

With the United States and the Soviet Union dominating world affairs as rivals, and each possessing nuclear-weapon technology, the world of the 1950s was locked in a Cold War between democracy and communism. The U.S.S.R., as well as the new communist government in China, promoted and supported the spread of communism in other nations by any means necessary, including war. In opposition, the U.S. and its allies were determined to support democratic governments worldwide.

> **"(The US and USSR) are like two scorpions in a bottle, each capable of killing the other but only at the risk of his own life...The atomic clock ticks faster and faster."**
>
> J. Robert Oppenheimer, 1956

Only five years after the end of World War II, the first major war of the nuclear age broke out when the communist North Korean army crossed the 38th parallel in June 1950 and invaded South Korea. The United Nations responded by sending in its forces, made up mostly of U.S. troops. Under the leadership of American General Douglas MacArthur, famous for his role as commander against Japan in World War II, the U.N. troops landed at Inchon in South Korea in September. By October 9 they had crossed the 38th parallel and pushed the North Korean forces out of South Korea.

Despite warnings from China that it would interfere, MacArthur continued his drive north until he reached the Chinese border at the Yalu River in November. Six days later China entered the war, and drove MacArthur's troops back out of North Korea by the end of the year. Contrary to President Harry S. Truman's wishes, MacArthur insisted on his plan for invading China, which led to Truman's firing the general in April 1951 for challenging presidential authority. Negotiations to end the war began in July, but no agreement was reached for another two years as the fighting continued. The Korean War armistice was finally signed in July 1953, leaving the borders much as they were before the conflict began. North and South Korea remained independent nations with a demilitarized zone (DMZ) along the border at the 38th parallel.

In response to the creation of NATO, the U.S.S.R and its Eastern European satellites signed a mutual defense treaty called the Warsaw Pact in 1955. To enforce this treaty, the Soviet Union stationed its troops within the borders of each signatory nation. Also in 1955, local rebellion drove France out of its colony of Indochina. The territory was then divided into the nations of Laos, Cambodia, North Vietnam, and South Vietnam. Under the leadership of Ho Chi Minh, North Vietnam became a communist state. The struggle between communist and anti-communist forces in South Vietnam would continue for two more decades. The Cold War further escalated when Cuban revolutionary leader Fidel Castro and his guerrillas deposed dictator Fulgencio Batista in 1959, and

FOR SALE

Small Farms—Out Beyond Atom Bombs

(1950 ad for property outside Washington, DC)

SKATEBOARD

Even in television's golden age, not everyone was a couch potato. A new form of outdoor entertainment arrived in 1958 with the invention of the skateboard. In Dana Point, California, surf-shop owner Bill Richards and his son Mark purchased a shipment of roller-skate-wheel assemblies from the Chicago Roller Skate Company and attached them to the bottom of wooden boards. Although primitive compared to today's skateboards, they offered a terrestrial alternative to surfing for only $8. In 1973 polyurethane wheels greatly improved maneuverability, and the skateboard's popularity began to skyrocket.

established the first communist government in the Western Hemisphere. Cuba's proximity to U.S. borders fueled the growth of anti-communist hysteria.

Although the U.S. and U.S.S.R. were not engaged in direct physical conflict with each other as in a conventional or "hot" war, the Cold War was a strong impetus for technological development. Each of the two leading world powers hoped to exert their political influences with the help of superior technology.

> "The Soviet government deems it necessary to report that the United States has no monopoly in the production of the hydrogen bomb."
>
> Soviet Premier Georgi Malenkov, 1953

With nations devoting massive resources to increasingly complex technological development, computers became a crucial element in the process. By performing complicated calculations in a fraction of the time taken by the most proficient humans, computers simplified important aspects of complicated endeavors and opened up new technological possibilities.

Technological rivalry between the U.S. and U.S.S.R. is perhaps most evident in the postwar nuclear-arms race. As devastating as the nuclear- fission bomb was, its power was dwarfed by the nuclear-fusion bomb developed by the U.S. in 1952. Also called the hydrogen bomb, or H-bomb, it did not remain a sole U.S. possession for long; the U.S.S.R. soon had its own hydrogen bombs, and the nuclear arms race achieved a new level of destructive potential.

The rivalry between the two nations' space programs was also intense. Outer space was a new and untapped frontier, and each country wanted to be the first to explore it. The Soviet Union took the early lead in this race when it sent the first manmade object into orbit, the satellite Sputnik, in 1957. The U.S. responded by launching its own probe into space, and the space race, like the arms race, would continue for decades.

Beyond the Sky's Limits

The stars have always been a source of wonder and mystery for humankind, but the study of the cosmos had always been confined to observations from within the earth's atmosphere. This began to change in the 1950s as rocketry began to be applied to space exploration, just as Konstantin Tsiolkovsky and Robert Goddard had envisioned decades before.

In order to travel into space, a vehicle must be able to escape the Earth's gravitational pull by attaining the appropriate speed, called the **"escape velocity."** To completely escape the earth's gravity in order to travel to the moon or other planets, a rocket must ascend at 25,000 miles an hour, or seven miles a second. To place a satellite into the Earth's orbit, a velocity of 17,500 miles an hour is required.

The rocket is the only known engine capable of producing enough energy to achieve such speeds. Rockets are also well suited for travel in the vacuum of space because they use an internal liquid oxidizer, unlike jet engines, which use oxygen from the air. The combination of fuel and oxidizer is called the **propellant**, and it usually represents 90 to 95 percent of the rocket's total weight.

There are several ways to maximize the efficiency of a rocket. A launch site close to the Equator is preferable because at that location, the gravitational pull is at its weakest. This is why American space missions depart from Cape Canaveral in Florida. It also helps to take off in an easterly direction to add the Earth's own velocity from its rotation. Rockets launched from Cape Canaveral gain an extra 900 miles an hour by doing this.

> **"Space isn't remote at all. It's only an hour's drive away if your car could go straight upwards."**
>
> Fred Hoyle, in the Observer, Sept. 9, 1979

CABLE TV

The first cable television service began with little attention on January 1, 1951, to 300 employees of the Zenith Radio Corporation in Chicago. Zenith Phonevision Service transmitted its signals through telephone lines, but a thicker "coaxial" cable later became the industry standard. Cable television did not gain widespread popularity until the early 1980s, when the Federal Communications Commission eased its regulations and allowed the industry to expand its audience to more than half of all households with televisions. Rather than receiving broadcast channels via antennae, cable TV customers could now view clearer pictures transmitted through a cable. Cable TV companies also provide dozens of additional channels — more than 100 in some areas — to customers who pay an installation charge and a monthly fee.

As Tsiolkovsky described in 1903, using multi-stage rockets, or stacking several rockets on top of each other, is an efficient way of escaping gravity. When the bottom rocket runs out of fuel and has accelerated to its top speed, it drops off as the second rocket fires up and takes over. This process continues through each stage. By lessening the total weight and boosting the next rocket to higher speeds, the spacecraft keeps accelerating throughout its flight. Most space rockets have three stages, but some have four.

After his surrender to American

troops, Wernher von Braun had established himself in the U.S. as a leading rocket expert. In 1950 the Army relocated him and his team of researchers, along with the confiscated German V-2 rockets, to their new headquarters at Redstone Arsenal at Huntsville, Alabama. With the start of the Korean War, the Army instructed von Braun to develop a mobile rocket with a 200-mile range for use in the field.

> **The American satellite should be called Civil Servant. It won't work, and you can't fire it.**
>
> Popular joke, 1957

The U.S. began taking space travel seriously in July 1952, when the National Advisory Committee for Aeronautics (NACA) passed a resolution to "devote modest efforts to problems of unmanned and manned flights at altitudes from 50 miles to infinity and at speeds from Mach 10 to escape from the Earth's gravity."

By this time, von Braun was working on the **Redstone** ballistic missile, applying much of the technology from the V-2 to fulfill the Army's requirements. The Redstone rocket's first test launch was August 20, 1953, and it traveled only 24,000 feet into the earth's atmosphere. Von Braun improved the Redstone over the next few years with plans for adapting it to space flight.

The U.S.S.R., meanwhile, had established a major rocket and space research program. In 1953, **Alexander Nesmayanov**, president of the Soviet Academy of Sciences, told the World Peace Council of his country's advancements.

"Science has reached a state when it is feasible to send a stratoplane to the moon," he said, "to create an artificial satellite of the Earth."

Despite this proclamation, most Americans underestimated the Soviet Union's scientific and technological capabilities and thought the U.S. would be the first to send a satellite into space. Most people were shocked when the U.S.S.R. beat the U.S. and successfully launched **Sputnik** into orbit. Although originally scheduled for launch on September 17, 1957, the 100th anniversary of Tsiolkovsky's birth, technical problems delayed the satellite's takeoff until October 4. It was still early enough for the U.S.S.R. to take the lead in the space race, an accomplishment it used to legitimize its political ideology.

After the successful flight, the Soviets announced, "The present generation will witness how the freed and conscious labor of the people of the new socialist society turns even the most daring of man's dreams into a reality."

The Sputnik satellite was a 184-pound steel sphere, 23 inches in diameter, with four flexible external antennae for radio transmissions of scientific data to the Russian Space Control Center near Moscow. It was launched into orbit by a rocket designed by engineer **Sergei P. Korolev**, often called the father of the Soviet space program. The government kept his identity highly classified, and the press officially referred to him as the Chief Designer of Launch Vehicles and Spacecraft. It was not until after his death in 1966 that Korolev's name was revealed to the public.

After circling the earth once every 96 minutes for 92 days, Sputnik burned up as it re-entered the atmosphere on January 4, 1958. While it was still in

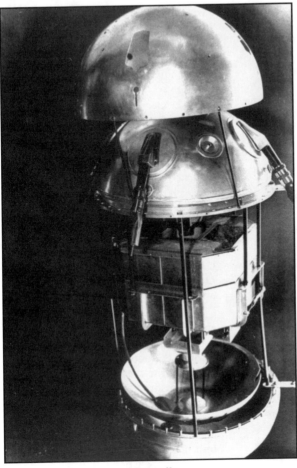

Sputnik

provided for Laika, the technology to return her from space did not exist, and Laika died from using up her air supply a week after leaving Earth. The dog's temporary survival, however, proved that life was possible in space. The Soviet Union was clearly planning to send a human into orbit.

These early Soviet successes prompted the U.S. to step up its efforts. Its first two launch attempts of Vanguard rockets by the U.S. Navy both ended in explosions on their launch pads. The press called these embarrassing incidents "Flopnik" and "Kaputnik." The Army's project, led by Wernher von Braun, was then given a chance.

Von Braun had already converted the Redstone missile for space flight, and named it **Jupiter**. After further modifications, the rocket was renamed **Juno**, and on January 31, 1958, it launched the first U.S. satellite into orbit. Although the 31-pound **Explorer I** satellite was much smaller than either of the two Sputniks, it made the first important scientific discovery of orbital research when it divulged the existence of two zones of charged particles in the Earth's magnetic field, called the **Van Allen Radiation Belts**.

After the U.S. Navy had worked out the glitches in its Vanguard rocket, the second American space probe was launched on March 17, 1958, two days after the Soviets launched the 2,866-

orbit, the Soviets launched a second satellite on November 3, 1957. **Sputnik 2** was about five times larger than its predecessor and contained the world's first living creature to travel into space, a female dog named **Laika**. Because of its canine cargo, the U.S. press called the probe "Muttnik." Monitoring equipment on-board showed that Laika survived the launch and suffered no adverse effects from weightlessness or other unknown space conditions. Although food was

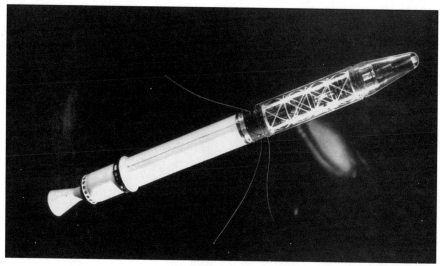

Explorer I

pound Sputnik 3. The **Vanguard I**, a sphere weighing only three pounds and measuring six inches in diameter, was nicknamed **"The Grapefruit."** Using data transmitted from Vanguard 1, American geophysicists determined that the Earth is not a perfect sphere.

Later that year, the U.S. decided to take its space program out of the military's hands and created a civilian agency, the **National Aeronautics and Space Administration (NASA)**, on October 1, 1958. With NASA in place, the U.S. initiated the **Mercury Project** on October 7, with the intention of sending manned spacecraft into orbit.

In December 1958 NASA launched a converted Air Force intercontinental ballistic missile (ICBM) into orbit. Unlike previous launches, in which multiple stages of rockets dropped off with only the satellite payload achieving orbit, the entire 8,600-pound Atlas rocket made it into space. Used to broadcast a recorded Christmas message by President Dwight

D. Eisenhower, the Atlas was a significant step forward in satellite communications.

"That's one of the astounding things again in this age of invention," Eisenhower said to reporters after hearing the transmission. "Maybe the next thing they'll do is televise pictures down here."

On January 2, 1959, the Soviet Union's space program set its sights even higher and launched **Luna I** aimed at Earth's only natural satellite, the moon. Luna I missed its mark and went into solar orbit, but it nevertheless became the first probe to completely escape the Earth's gravity. **Luna 2** was more accurate and became the first manmade object to complete the 236,875 mile voyage when it crash-landed on the moon near the Sea of Serenity on September 12, 1959. The following month, **Luna 3** offered the first glimpse of the "dark side" of the moon, never seen from Earth because of equal periods of rotation and revolution. The photographs

The Mercury Seven test pilots

were automatically processed on-board and televised back to Earth.

The Ultimate Weapon

As the decade drew to a close, the space race was in high gear, and both nations were competing to put the first man into space. Unlike the space race, the nuclear-arms race was a competition for sheer destructive power.

After the U.S. demonstrated the annihilating potential of atomic bombs with the devastation of Hiroshima and Nagasaki, many considered nuclear- fission explosives to be the ultimate weapon. Even before Otto Hahn split the first uranium nucleus, scientists had begun exploring the possibility of small nuclei joining together, or fusing, to form larger nuclei. **Fission** splits nuclei of the

heaviest elements into lighter ones, while **fusion** welds together the nuclei of the lightest element, hydrogen, into the heavier helium.

American physicist Hans Bethe published a theory in 1938 stating that the heat from the sun and other stars is produced by the fusion of hydrogen atoms into helium. Extreme high temperatures in the range of 40 million degrees Celsius are necessary to achieve a fusion reaction. With the recent introduction of the fission bomb, this temperature range became accessible, and the **hydrogen bomb** became a technological possibility. By surrounding a normal atomic-fission bomb with hydrogen, the explosion would generate the required heat to trigger a fusion reaction and create a blast hundreds or even thousands of times more powerful than the fission bomb alone. Because heat initiates the reaction, hydrogen bombs are also called **thermonuclear weapons**.

The Soviet Union's acquisition of the atomic bomb in 1949 prompted the U.S. to seriously consider developing the more powerful hydrogen bomb. Thinking the U.S.S.R. was close to developing its own fusion weapon, President Harry S. Truman approved the project in January 1950, to be headed by physicist **Edward Teller**, a Hungarian émigré who had worked on the Manhattan Project.

The U.S. tested the first thermonuclear bomb on November 1, 1952, at

> **"The immediate cause of World War III is the preparation of it."**
>
> C. Wright Mills, 1959

114

Eniwetok atoll in the South Pacific. The power of its explosion was equivalent to 10 million tons (10 megatons) of TNT and was 500 times more powerful than the first atomic bombs. The successful detonation put the U.S. ahead in the ominous arms race, but only briefly, because the Soviet Union detonated its own hydrogen bomb the following year. Able to easily destroy the world's largest cities, the hydrogen bomb proved to be the ultimate weapon, and to this day comprises the bulk of each side's nuclear arsenal.

With the ultimate weapon in each superpower's possession, the next step was to develop effective delivery systems and more bombs. Before long each rival had the ability to destroy the planet many times over.

Rocket technology was applicable to the space race and the arms race. The same rockets used to send probes into space could also be used as ICBMs to deliver nuclear weapons to targets anywhere on Earth. The U.S.S.R. did in fact have operational ICBMs by the time of Sputnik's launch in 1957. The U.S. successfully tested its first ICBM, the Air Force's Atlas missile with a 9,000-mile range, in December of that year.

As Enrico Fermi's first nuclear reactor demonstrated in 1942, the destructive power of a nucleus is also a tremendous source of energy. Nuclear reactors have been providing power to industrialized nations for decades. Although there are many different designs for nuclear power plants, most operate under the same basic principles. The nuclear reaction, with its intensity regulated by neutron-absorbing control rods, continuously heats a liquid into steam in the reactor's central core. Like coal or oil, the reactor's main purpose is to produce a gas to turn a turbine that drives a power generator. One gram of uranium can generate as much power as two tons of oil.

One of the nuclear reactor's first applications was as a power source for a new breed of submarine. When the U.S. Navy introduced the nuclear-powered **Nautilus** in 1957, many considered it to be the world's first true submarine. Dependent on oxygen to drive their generators, earlier submarines could travel only limited distances underwater and at reduced speeds. While submerged, nuclear-powered submarines, on the other hand, have virtually no limit as to how far they can travel and can move faster than many surface ships. The Nautilus demonstrated its underwater range

The nuclear powered Nautilus submarine

TRANSISTOR RADIO
— — — — — — — — —

The transistor's first commercial application was to make a smaller hearing aid in 1953, but its use in radios made it famous. Indianapolis-based Regency Electronics released the first transistor radio, the TR-1, for the Christmas season in 1954. The transistor allowed the radio to be small enough to fit into a pocket, and it was an instant success. Tokyo Telecommunications Engineering Corporation produced the first Japanese transistor radio, the Sony, in August 1955. It was also highly successful, and the company changed its name to Sony in 1957. By the end of the 1950s various Japanese electronic companies had established their dominance in the transistor-radio market all over the world.

1954 pocket radio

in 1958 by traveling from the U.S. to Europe under the Arctic icecaps of the North Pole. It used 2.8 pounds of uranium to power it through its first 62,000 miles; a conventionally powered submarine would require 720,000 gallons of oil for a voyage of equivalent distance.

Around the same time, much larger nuclear reactors began generating power on land. The U.S.S.R. began operating the world's first nuclear reactor for civilian use in June 1954. Similar plants in the U.S. and Great Britain went into use soon after. Nuclear power plants need to be near a large water supply in order to effectively cool the reactors, and therefore are often situated on coastlines, wide estuaries, or large lakes. Riverside locations, however, are undesirable because the moist ground cannot support a plant's tremendous weight. The reactor alone can weigh up to 50,000 tons, while the surrounding pressure vessel and necessary shielding can weigh an additional 200,000 tons. The foundation also weighs thousands of tons and must be laid with extreme accuracy. Nuclear power plants are generally also limited to areas far from large populations in order to prevent potential radioactive accidents from inflicting widespread human contamination.

Although kept secret until 1989, one of the earliest serious accidents involving nuclear power occurred in 1957 at a Soviet nuclear-weapons plant in the Ural Mountains. After a tank of radioactive waste exploded, releasing large amounts of radiation, the surrounding area, equivalent in size to the state of Rhode Island, had to be abandoned until 1974 because the accident left it so heavily contaminated.

Nuclear power is a very productive and efficient source of energy, but fission

SOLAR CELL

In 1886 Charles Fritts invented the solar photovoltaic (PV) cell, using selenium to convert the sun's energy into electricity. Although it was inefficient, the device worked. Still, the scientific world refused to believe in what appeared to be "free energy," and wrote Fritts off as a fraud. The PV cell remained in obscurity until 1954, when Daryl Chapin, Gerald Pearson, and Calvin Fuller of AT&T's Bell Laboratories developed a semiconductor solar cell that was five times more efficient than its selenium predecessor. The Bell scientists continued to increase their silicon cells' efficiency, and in 1958 NASA used them to provide electricity for its Vanguard I satellite. All NASA satellites since that time have employed solar cells to convert the sun's rays into electricity. Solar energy is a safe and renewable energy source but is still too expensive for widespread use on Earth. Photovoltaic cells are commonly used in small electronic devices such as calculators and watches, as well as in larger arrays in areas lacking a conventional energy source.

also creates entirely new types of radioactive substances, many of which can be extremely harmful. These byproducts can cause the mutation of genetic materials in living cells. If an exposed plant or animal survives the initial exposure to radiation, it could hand down a mutated genetic code to its offspring and subsequent generations.

The main byproduct of a nuclear weapon is **fallout**, the collection of radioactive substances falling from the sky after the nuclear explosion. Many of the people involved in the Manhattan Project later contracted cancer from exposure to fallout and other sources of radiation. A nuclear reactor, however, is designed to produce a controlled reaction. It retains the lethal materials in its body, protected by a special shield and a complex system of safety measures. The disposal of this radioactive waste is perhaps the most serious problem of nuclear power.

Zeroes and Ones

Many of the advances in space and nuclear technologies would not have been possible without computers to perform the increasingly complex calculations necessary for these endeavors.

The transistor eliminated the need for vacuum tubes, and solved some of the major problems associated with the early computers such as the Colossus and ENIAC.

In order to avoid disassembling a computer and rewiring it for different procedures or programs, as was necessary with previous computers, Hungarian-American mathematician **John von Neumann** proposed the concept of the **stored program**, a system in which a program is coded in the same way as stored data and can remain in the computer as long as needed. This would allow the user to instruct the computer to change programs without taking it apart.

To further simplify computers, von Neumann proposed the use of a **binary operating system** rather than the decimal system normally used by humans as well as ENIAC. The decimal system uses 10 digits for counting — the same number of digits, or fingers, we have on our hands. By using the simpler binary system, any number can be expressed with two digits — zero and one. If an electric pulse represents the number one, and the absence of a pulse represents zero, computers can then perform any function based on a succession of existing and non-existing electric pulses, which can be generated very quickly.

The binary, or **digital**, system was applied to computers based on a system of logic more than 100 years old. In the 1840s, English mathematician **George Boole** stated that any decision, regardless of complexity, could be reduced to two variables. In other words, ones and zeros could symbolize either yes or no, positive or negative, on or off. Although few people paid much attention to Boolean logic during its creator's lifetime, it proved to be an effective system

for computers and remains the standard to this day.

Von Neumann also described other principles that would become industry standards for digital electronic computers, including such components as a central arithmetical unit, a central control unit to instruct the computer in its actions and their order, a memory storage unit, an input device, an output device, and a recording device.

The first computer to employ von Neumann's principles and Boolean logic was **EDVAC** (Electronic Discrete Variable Calculator), completed in 1950 by the same men who had built **ENIAC**, **John Mauchly** and **John P. Eckert**. The University of Pennsylvania researchers later formed the Mauchly Eckert Computer Company to manufacture and sell computers, and in 1951 they completed **UNIVAC** (Universal Automatic Computer), the first commercial computer to be widely available, as well as the first to use magnetic tape for storage of up to one million characters. It also had an internal memory capacity of 1,000 12-digit binary numbers and could calculate 2,000 additions or 450 multiplications per second. The U.S. Census Bureau bought the first UNIVAC, but businesses were initially reluctant to buy the million-dollar computers. Financial difficulties forced Mauchly and Eckert

UNIVAC

Kilby's Integrated circuit

to sell their company to the typewriter manufacturer Remington Rand.

UNIVAC became famous during the American presidential elections of 1952. On a Columbia Broadcasting System (CBS) national broadcast hosted by Walter Cronkite, UNIVAC predicted that Dwight D. Eisenhower would win with 438 electoral votes several hours before the official tabulations became available and based on only seven percent of the returns. The computer's prediction turned out to be extremely accurate, as Eisenhower beat Adlai Stevenson by winning 432 electoral votes. As amazing as this this achievement appeared, computers can do only what humans instruct them to do. UNIVAC simply calculated a series of complex formulas entered by a group of engineers and political scientists to come up with the final result.

The election-night telecast dramatically increased awareness and confidence in UNIVAC, and in 1954, General Electric (GE) became the first large U.S. corporation to purchase the machine for use in its accounting department. Remington Rand eventually sold 50 UNIVAC computers.

Overthrowing the Tyranny of Numbers

Other computers followed, and some began incorporating transistors rather than vacuum tubes. Although the transistor revolutionized the electronics industry, it also created a whole new set of problems for engineers. A transistor works as part of an electronic circuit, where all the components are made separately and wired together. Increasingly

Jack Kilby

Electrical engineer **Jack Kilby** of Texas Instruments in Dallas made the first integrated circuit by combining the main components of a circuit — transistors, resistors, and capacitors — and implanting them into a single chip of the semiconductor germanium connected by tiny gold wires. Meanwhile, physicist **Robert Noyce**, formed his own company, called Fairchild Semiconductor, in Mountain View, California. Noyce had also made an integrated circuit, but he used the **"planar process,"** which established connections between electrical components by sandwiching them between the layers of semiconductors, thus eliminating the need for wires. Kilby and Texas Instruments soon had a similar idea and also developed a chip without wires. Both applied for patents in 1959, a matter that took 10 years of legal battles to settle. Noyce ended up winning the case in 1969, but by that time the two companies had cross-licensed each other and both collected royalties from other chip manufacturers. Kilby and Noyce considered themselves the co-inventors of the integrated circuit, as did the rest of the industry.

The integrated circuit was a major breakthrough in electronics and led to the production of smaller and cheaper computers, which ultimately allowed them to become a tool not just for research laboratories and military equipment, but for everyone. Chips have become an integral part of almost anything electronic all over the world, from jet fighters and space stations to wristwatches and video games.

complex equipment required more and smaller circuits which made it difficult to put together. Engineers called the phenomenon the **"tyranny of numbers,"** and it threatened to stall further progress in electronic development.

The U.S. military and space program, in need of reliable miniaturized electronics and computers capable of guiding missiles and space rockets, distributed millions of dollars in funding to find a way of overthrowing the tyranny of numbers. The revolution came in 1958 with the invention of the **integrated circuit** (IC), or chip. Once again, two independent inventors were responsible.

Entertainment Technology

The first video game was completed the same year as the integrated circuit. Physicist **Willy Higinbotham**, another former member of the Manhattan Project team, was working for Brookhaven National Laboratory in Upton, New York, in 1958 when he had the idea for a computerized game. After he connected a cathode-ray tube (CRT) to a laboratory computer, a bouncing ball appeared on the screen. Higinbotham began assembling spare electronic parts to rig a way of controlling the ball.

"We looked around and found that we had a few pieces we could throw together and make a game which would have a ball bouncing back and forth, sort of like a tennis game viewed from the side," he recalled.

Two weeks later the game was up and running. In the center of the round five-inch screen was a horizontal line representing the surface of the tennis court, and a shorter vertical line extended upward from its center, representing the net. Each of two players used a box with a button and a knob as controls. Pushing the button "hit" the ball to the other end of the court, and the knob controlled how high the ball was hit. There were no paddles on the screen, but if the ball hit the net it would bounce back — a high-tech effect for 1958.

"People want their movies the way they are — not on TV."

Harry Cohn of Columbia Pictures, (1954)

At the laboratory's annual open house, visitors waited in long lines to play the new game, much to Higinbotham's surprise; it didn't seem like a big deal to him. By the next year's open house in 1959, Higinbotham had increased the screen size to 15 inches and modified the game to simulate tennis on the moon with very low gravity or on Jupiter with a much stronger gravitational pull. Visitors again lined up to play

1955 Stratosphere from Zenith

it, but despite the game's success at the open houses, Higinbotham never made any money from it, for he never patented or marketed it. He felt that the idea was so simple that anyone could have made it, but no one else did. Much later, in 1971, Atari released a very similar game called **Pong**, which became very popular and introduced video games to the general public.

> **"If the television craze continues with the present level of programs, we are destined to have a nation of morons."**
>
> Boston University president Daniel Marsh, 1950

The most popular source of entertainment in the 1950s was television. By 1956 almost 72 percent of American homes had a set to watch popular shows such as "I Love Lucy" and "The Honeymooners." Television sets and broadcasts had only been in black-and-white, but two rival systems of color television were vying for acceptance as the industry standard in the early part of the decade. CBS had introduced a high-quality color broadcasting system in 1953, but it was incompatible with existing black-and-white television sets. RCA, which owned the National Broadcasting Company (NBC), responded with its own system the following year. The quality of the picture was not as good as CBS' color system, but RCA's advantage was that black-and-white televisions could receive the new color transmissions. The Federal Communications Commission decided to adopt the RCA system so the public would not be forced to purchase new color television sets to receive broadcasts. Color television pro-

grams would not be regularly broadcast, however, until the 1960s.

Television was well on its way to becoming a powerful medium for entertainment and information. The space race of the 1950s offered a glimpse of the future role of satellites in communications. Meanwhile, the development of the hydrogen bomb and the heightening of the arms race kept the public's attention on broadcasting for the latest developments. During the 1952 presidential elections television revealed the impressive capabilities of UNIVAC. The subsequent invention of the integrated circuit helped transform computers into powerful machines driving development in various technological fields.

TECHNOLOGY

chapter 7

1960-1969
Exploring New Worlds

Edwin Aldrin on the moon, July 21, 1969

Since the evolution of human life, people have colonized and explored every corner of the Earth's land mass. In the 1960s, the first humans left the planet, to open a new frontier for exploration and possible colonization. Space travel captured the imaginations of people all over the world as the U.S. and U.S.S.R. competed to achieve new milestones. The Soviets retained their early lead in the space race by sending the first man into orbit in 1961, but the U.S. made up ground quickly and landed men on the moon in 1969.

On earth, the Cold War rivalry intensified rapidly as the decade unfolded. In May 1960, Soviet fighters shot down a high-altitude American U-2 reconnaissance plane flying over the U.S.S.R. The surviving pilot, Francis Gary Powers, was caught, convicted of espionage, and imprisoned for two years until the U.S. traded a captured Soviet spy for his release. In the divided city of Berlin, the communist East German government built the Berlin Wall in August 1961 to prevent refugees from fleeing to the West.

Closer to home, the U.S. severed diplomatic relations with Cuba in January 1961 after Fidel Castro's newly established communist regime nationalized the country's banks and industries, including American-owned property worth hundreds of millions of dollars. The U.S. then imposed a trade embargo on Cuba. In April, a small force of Cuban exiles trained by the U.S. Central Intelligence Agency (CIA) landed on their home island at the Bay of Pigs. Contrary to the CIA's expectations, it did not inspire the Cuban population to rise in rebellion. Castro's army easily defeated the invaders, leaving an embarrassing fiasco for President John F. Kennedy, who

> **"Once the rockets are up, who cares where they come down? That's not my department."**
>
> Wernher von Braun

accepted full responsibility.

After U.S. aerial photographs revealed the construction of Soviet missile bases in Cuba, Kennedy announced a naval blockade of the island in October 1962 to prevent the delivery of further arms from the U.S.S.R. As Soviet ships approached, tensions increased dramatically, and the ensuing Cuban Missile Crisis was the closest the world ever came to a nuclear war. Five days later, the U.S.S.R. agreed to remove its missiles from Cuba if the U.S. withdrew its missiles from Turkey, and World War III was avoided.

With North Vietnam already established as a communist state under leader Ho Chi Minh, the U.S. increased its support for South Vietnam in its domestic conflict against the north's communist revolutionaries, the Viet Cong. Both the U.S. and North Vietnam had initially been supplying their respective allies in South Vietnam with equipment and military advisors, but in December 1963 the North Vietnamese army began its own operations in the south. American involvement escalated in August 1964 when North Vietnamese patrol boats attacked a U.S. Navy destroyer in the international waters of the Tonkin Gulf. Within days, American planes began bombing North Vietnam in retaliation. Overwhelmingly, Congress approved the Tonkin Gulf Resolution, giving then President Lyndon B. Johnson virtual freedom to handle the entire situation as he saw fit. The U.S. sent in its first combat troops in March 1965, and although

Congress never officially declared war, the Vietnam conflict became the longest military engagement in American history.

With stockpiles of nuclear weapons growing on both sides of the Cold War and the potential danger of nuclear fallout becoming more evident, the U.S., U.S.S.R., and Great Britain signed an agreement in August 1963 prohibiting nuclear-weapons testing in the Earth's atmosphere, in space, and underwater, but continuing to allow underground detonations. Around the same time, the U.S. and the U.S.S.R. established a direct telephone link, or "hot line," connecting the two capitals, at the White House and the Kremlin, to improve communications between the leaders of each superpower. Shortly after helping to establish this communication link, President Kennedy was assassinated in Dallas on November 22, 1963.

The space race between the two nations had a tremendous impact on improving communications throughout the world as specialized satellites became highly effective tools for broadcasting and telephone connections. From their strategic vantage points in orbit, satellites were also very useful for predicting weather on Earth. The 1960s also saw the introduction of the laser, an extremely useful tool with vastly diverse applications, in heavy industry, medicine and communications. In the minds of the majority of the world's population, the most awe-inspiring technological achievement of the decade, and perhaps of the century, was humankind's first successful journey to the moon.

Lunar Orbiter 1, 1966

Steps and Leaps

From the beginning of the decade, the objective of the U.S. space program was clear. On May 25, 1961, less than four years after Sputnik became the first manmade object to travel into space, President Kennedy directed NASA to shoot for the moon.

"I believe that this nation should commit itself to achieving the goal, before this decade is out, of landing a man on the moon and returning him safely to the Earth," the president declared.

NASA had significant work ahead of it to fulfill Kennedy's goal, for at this point American astronauts had not even achieved orbit around the Earth. Before attempting to send a man into space, the problem of returning him safely to Earth

"The view is out of this world."

Astronaut Edwin "Buzz" Aldrin said of the sight of the receding earth on the way to the moon

had to be solved. Since the friction caused by a spacecraft falling through the Earth's atmosphere produces enough heat to incinerate it and its contents, some form of protection had to be devised.

The U.S.S.R. solved this problem by attaching a heat shield with a special protective coating to dissipate the heat during re-entry. The launch of **Sputnik 5** on August 19, 1960, demonstrated the concept. Carrying two dogs, mice, rats, houseflies, and plants, the satellite orbited Earth 18 times before returning safely home with its passengers alive. It was the first successful recovery of a spacecraft from orbit.

Both nations worked feverishly to propel the first human into space, and again the Soviet Union prevailed, maintaining its lead in the space race. With cosmonaut **Yuri Gagarin** on board, **Vostok 1** left Earth on April 12, 1961. Weighing more than 10,000 pounds, the capsule had a pressurized and air-conditioned cabin with equipment to monitor Gagarin's physiological reactions to the flight. A television system provided visual monitoring of the cabin's interior. Retro-

rockets on the capsule controlled re-entry speed. After orbiting once in 108 minutes, Vostok 1's retro-rocket fired and directed it back to Earth. Gagarin ejected from the capsule when it fell to an altitude of about two miles, and safely parachuted to the ground.

Less than a month later, the U.S. attempted its first manned space flight as part of NASA's Mercury program. Piloted by **Alan Shepard, Jr.** the **Freedom 7** capsule was launched into space on May 5, 1961, and although it did not achieve orbit, it was an important step forward in America's space program. Another suborbital flight followed in July with **Virgil "Gus" Grissom** on board. Both flights reached altitudes of more than 100 miles and were recovered safely after splashing down in the Atlantic Ocean.

Before the U.S. could place its first astronaut into orbit, the U.S.S.R. launched **Vostok 2** on August 6, 1961, with cosmonaut **Gherman S. Titov**. Vostok 2 orbited the Earth 17 times, and after spending more than 25 hours in space it returned Titov safely home. While in orbit, he experienced nausea caused by prolonged weightlessness, but he began to recover as he re-entered the atmosphere. Although Titov felt fine upon his return, the episode revealed the need to devote more research to the effects of weightlessness.

The next manned Mercury mission took off on February 20, 1962, launching **John Glenn** and his capsule **Friendship 7** into orbit. Glenn stayed in space for nearly five hours and orbited the Earth three times before attempting re-entry. At this point, ground control noticed that the capsule's heat shield may have come loose. With the capsule and its pilot in danger of incineration, the

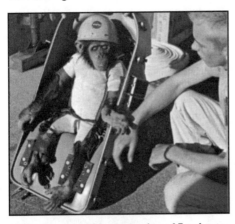

Chimp named Ham survives 15 minute space flight, 1961

decision was made to leave the retro-rocket pack attached rather than releasing it as planned, with hopes that its straps would hold the heat shield in place. The retro-rockets burned away during re-entry, but the heat shield maintained its position, and Glenn made it back safely. In a New York ticker-tape parade following the historic flight, millions of people honored Glenn for becoming the first American to orbit the Earth. The event was reminiscent of the reception Charles Lindbergh received after his historic New York-to-Paris flight in 1927.

After a total of seven flights, Project Mercury ended on May 16, 1963, with the re-entry of **Leroy Gordon Cooper Jr.** from a 22-orbit mission lasting more than 34 hours. The following month, the Soviet launch of **Vostok 6** made its pilot, **Valentina Tereshkova**, the first

The Mercury Redstone

woman in space.

The U.S.S.R. initiated its Voskhod program on October 12, 1964. With three cosmonauts on board, **Voskhod I** was the first spacecraft to carry multiple passengers. Launched on March 18, 1965, **Voskhod 2's** mission was to complete the first spacewalk. With an air supply in a tank on his back, cosmonaut **Aleksei Leonov** entered an airlock, depressurized it, and drifted into space through the outer hatch. Connected to the ship by only a fragile lifeline, Leonov spent 20 minutes in space photographing the Earth and the spacecraft, while suffering no ill effects. Technical problems during re-entry, however, forced Voskhod 2 to land off course in a remote snowy region of the U.S.S.R., hundreds of miles from its intended landing area. Leonov and fellow cosmonaut **Pavel Belayev** had no choice but to build a fire and spent the night in the frosty wilderness until their rescuers came the next day.

The two Voskhod flights came before

> **"It was quite a day. I don't know what you can say about a day when you see four beautiful sunsets."**
>
> John Glenn after first American orbital flight 1962

Glenn orbits earth, 1962

the U.S. could launch its first Gemini mission. Gemini's main purpose was to perfect designs and techniques to be used in a future moon landing. This included sending two astronauts into space, a rendezvous and docking with another spacecraft, and spacewalking.

After two unmanned Gemini flights, **Gemini 3** took off on March 23, 1965—only five days after Voskhod 2. On board were **John Young** and Mercury veteran **Virgil Grissom**, who had managed to smuggle a corned-beef sandwich on board with him.

Launched on June 3, 1965, the **Gemini 4** mission was televised internationally because it was to include the first American spacewalk, or extravehicular activity (**EVA**). While orbiting the Earth at nearly 18,000 miles per hour, astronaut **Edward White** propelled himself through space with a hand-held maneuvering unit for 21 minutes before re-entering the spaceship.

"It (the end of the spacewalk) was the saddest moment of my life," White later said.

The U.S. began to catch up in the space race when **Gemini 8** performed the world's first space docking with an Agena target vehicle on March 16, 1966. About 20 minutes after successfully completing the procedure, astronauts **Neil Armstrong** and **David Scott** reported that both spacecraft had begun to spin uncontrollably. Thinking the problem was with the target vehicle, the astronauts separated from the Agena, but the spinning only increased to a rate of about one revolution per second. Approaching unconsciousness, Armstrong activated the re-entry system and regained control of the ship. After 11 hours of what was supposed to be a three-day mission, Gemini 8 made an emergency landing in the Pacific Ocean. An investigation revealed that a faulty maneuvering thruster, stuck in the open position, caused the spacecraft to spin.

By the time of **Gemini 12's** return to Earth, marking the end of the project, American astronauts had completed several successful spacewalks and dockings. NASA was now ready to start the **Apollo** project to fulfill John F. Kennedy's goal of sending an American to the moon.

After five failed Soviet attempts, the **Luna 9** unmanned probe became the first spacecraft to land safely on the moon when it "soft-landed" in the Ocean of Storms on February 3, 1966. Luna 9 also televised the first pictures of the moon's surface.

Gemini 4 astronaut Edward White's EVA

That same year, NASA followed with its own soft landing of **Surveyor 1** on June 2, and in 1967, **Surveyor 6** lifted off from the lunar surface, flew to a different location, and landed safely. It was the first time an engine had been restarted on a celestial body. The Surveyor missions provided important information about the lunar surface and its ability to support a landing.

Wernher von Braun designed the Apollo spacecraft to accommodate three astronauts, two of whom would descend to the moon in a detachable lightweight **Lunar Module** (LM), while one remained in orbit in the combined **Command and Service Module** (CSM). To propel the Apollo craft to the moon, NASA would use von Braun's Saturn 5 three-stage rocket. Longer than a football field, the 363-foot-tall Saturn 5 was the largest and most powerful rocket ever launched and was vital to the success of the mission. The preliminary Apollo missions leading up to the moon landing used the Saturn 1B rocket until it was replaced by the Saturn 5 in December 1968 for the **Apollo 8** mission.

The Apollo program got off to a tragic start in 1967. During a training exercise on January 27 for the scheduled February 21 liftoff, **Apollo 1** astronauts **Roger Chaffee**, **Edward White**, and **Virgil Grissom** were sealed in the spacecraft on the launch pad when a fire broke out in the cockpit. Because the capsule's interior contained pure oxygen, it instantly incinerated, killing all three astronauts. Grissom, White, and Chaffee became the first astronauts to die on the job. Investigators later determined that an electrical malfunction had caused the spark that started the fire. To avoid similar tragedies, NASA decided to use a gas mixture less combustible than pure oxygen for future space missions. The

The Apollo 11 crew
(l. to r.) Aldrin, Armstrong and Collins

disaster significantly delayed the continuation of the Apollo project.

Only three months later, the Soviet space program had a disaster of its own during the **Soyuz 1** mission. During its descent on April 24, the Soyuz spacecraft crashed to Earth after its parachute malfunctioned. Cosmonaut **Vladimir Komarov** became the first person to die during a space mission. The tragedy, as well as the death of chief designer **Sergei Korolev** the previous year, significantly set back the Soviet space program. Its next manned spaceflight came on October 26, 1968, with the launch of **Soyuz 3**.

After several unmanned missions, **Apollo 7** became the first piloted flight of the program on October 11, 1968. During 163 Earth orbits in 11 days, the astronauts tested the new equipment

NEIL ARMSTRONG'S MISQUOTE:

■ ■ ■ ■ ■ ■ ■ ■ ■

"That's one small step for (a) man, one giant leap for mankind."

As the world was watching astronaut Neil Armstrong take his historic first step onto the surface of the moon, the radio transmission of his spoken statement was distorted by static, and many people did not hear him say the article "a" before the word "man." The majority of the media heard it the same way and incorrectly reported the famous quote as "That's one small step for man, one giant leap for mankind," which is how most people still remember it.

and routines for the upcoming moon landing. Launched on December 21 with the new Saturn 5 rocket, **Apollo 8** sent the first humans into lunar orbit. The three astronauts completed 10 orbits and returned to Earth on December 27. The **Apollo 9** mission in March 1969 successfully tested the separation and re-docking of the Lunar Module in Earth's orbit. With each mission taking the U.S. a step closer to a moon landing, the final test was **Apollo 10**. After lifting off on May 18, astronauts brought the Lunar Module to within nine miles of the moon's surface. Apollo 10 splashed down in the Pacific Ocean on May 26, and NASA prepared for the final step.

On the morning of July 16, 1969, with much of the world watching the event on television, Apollo 11 left the Earth to take **Neil Armstrong, Edwin "Buzz" Aldrin**, and **Michael Collins** to the moon. After achieving lunar orbit three days later, Armstrong described the view of the moon: "It looks very much like the pictures but like the difference between watching a real football game and one on TV. There's no substitute for actually being here."

On July 20, Armstrong and Aldrin entered the Lunar Module, the **"Eagle"** and successfully separated from the Command and Service Module, the **"Columbia"**. Collins stayed aboard the Columbia to pilot the "mother ship" in orbit while Armstrong and Aldrin explored the moon's surface.

"The Eagle has wings," Armstrong reported to Mission Control in Houston.

During the 12-minute descent into the **Sea of Tranquility**, the automatic guidance system, controlled by a computer using integrated circuits, was about to land the Eagle into a large field of boulders. When Armstrong realized what was happening, he took manual control of the craft and landed it safely about four miles away just before the allocated landing fuel ran out.

"Houston, Tranquility Base here," Armstrong said to Mission Control as history's largest television audience watched. "The Eagle has landed."

His voice was calm, but at 156 beats per minute, his heart was beating at twice its usual rate. Armstrong and Aldrin were anxious to begin their moonwalk. After taking six and a half hours to perform the necessary preliminary procedures, they depressurized the cabin and opened the hatch. Armstrong was the first to exit, and as he became the first human to set foot on the moon, he spoke his famous words to the

AUDIOCASSETTE

The phonograph record had been the primary medium for recorded music since Thomas Edison patented it in 1877. In 1962 the Dutch company Philips introduced the compact audiocassette, which soon began to compete with the LP (long-playing record). Unlike records, audiocassettes offered the option of recording onto them, something only reel-to-reel tapes could previously do. Predominantly used by professionals, reel-to-reel tapes were complicated, unwieldy, and expensive. Cassettes, on the other hand, were easy to use, compact, and economical. Playback, rewind, and fast-forward were controlled by just a push of a button, and the tape could be stopped and ejected at any point. A cassette's housing protected it from wear and made it safe and easy to handle, which helped keep the sound quality from deteriorating.

world: "That's one small step for (a) man, one giant leap for mankind."

Almost an hour later, Aldrin exited the spaceship to join Armstrong in conducting experiments and collecting almost 50 pounds of lunar rock and soil samples. A couple of hours later, the two men boarded the Eagle and returned to the Columbia, waiting in orbit to take them home. They left behind an American flag (which would never wave in the windless environment of the moon) and a plaque signed by all three astronauts as well as President Richard M. Nixon.

"Here men from the planet Earth first set foot upon the moon July 1969 A.D.," the plaque read. "We came in peace for all mankind."

The U.S. had succeeded in fulfilling the late President Kennedy's challenge of landing a man on the moon and returning him safely to Earth before the end of the decade. It was one of the most remarkable events in all of history. The decade witnessed a second lunar landing by humans, with the launch of **Apollo 12** in November.

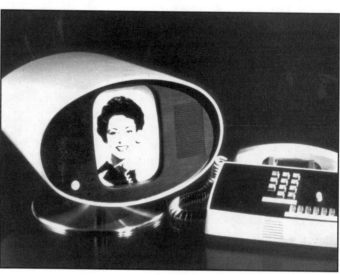

The AT&T Picturephone, 1964

The Tiros Satellite

"I think it is equal in importance to that moment in evolution when aquatic life came crawling up on the land," Werner von Braun said of the accomplishment he helped make possible.

Technology had finally allowed humans to travel to an extraterrestrial world. The moon, along with the sun, is the most significant object in the solar system to life on Earth. It is the brightest light in the night sky and the mysterious force governing our orbit, the motion of the oceans, and the eternal inspiration for earthbound poets and artists.

Maximizing Space

While piloted exploration was the most glamorous aspect of the space race, unmanned satellites with various purposes provided unprecedented levels of utility for the vast majority of the world's population.

Although the telephone had been invented in the previous century, as late as 1956 the only way to speak to someone across the Atlantic Ocean was by radiotelephone. The system was unreliable, as poor weather often interrupted these calls. The first trans-Atlantic telephone cable was laid across the ocean floor that year, but it was limited by the number of calls that it could handle. With new technology capable of launching objects into space, new approaches to communications became feasible.

In 1945 British science-fiction writer **Arthur C. Clarke** first described the possibility of establishing an effective worldwide telecommunications network by utilizing a network of orbiting satellites. At an altitude of 22,300 miles over the Equator, the satellites would orbit the Earth once every 24 hours. Since this is also the rate of the planet's revolution, the satellites would remain over the same spot on the Earth's surface,

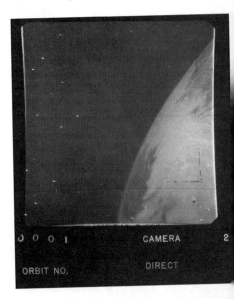

Picture of earth from the Tiros Satellite

132

LIGHT-EMITTING DIODE
— — — — — — — — — —

Introduced in 1962, the LED (light-emitting diode) is a semiconductor device used to emit a visible light meant only to be seen, rather than to illuminate like a light bulb. LEDs are often small colored lights used in calculator displays and countless other electronic components to indicate settings, such as whether a mechanism is on or off.

which is why this particular altitude is called **"geosynchronous"** or **"geostationary"** orbit.

Inspired by Clarke, AT&T's Bell Laboratories engineer **John R. Pierce** wrote several theoretical articles about the use of satellites for communications in the early 1950s. After the U.S. began launching man made satellites into orbit, Pierce approached NASA and presented his ideas for communications satellites.

On April 12, 1960, NASA launched **Echo 1**, a metallic balloon 100 feet in diameter, into low orbit to test the feasibility of Pierce's concept. As a passive reflector satellite, Echo 1 bounced radio waves transmitted from Earth to distant locations. The test proved successful on the satellite's second orbit when it reflected a transmission of President Eisenhower's voice from California to New Jersey.

The following year, Bell Labs began work on an active communications satellite, one which could transmit as well as receive signals. The result was **Telstar**, the world's first commercial communications satellite; it could handle 600 telephone calls simultaneously or one television transmission. Great Britain and

France began to build satellite receiving stations of their own.

AT&T paid NASA to launch Telstar 1 into space, and on the early morning of July 10, 1962, the 35-inch spherical satellite achieved orbit. Later that day, Telstar 1 began relaying a trans-Atlantic television transmission from the U.S. to France. Telstar 1 remained in operation until February 1963, when a high-altitude atomic explosion damaged some of its transistors just months before an international treaty outlawing such detonations was signed.

Although it was a vast improvement over the radiotelephone, Telstar 1's low orbit limited its effectiveness, because it was in range of ground stations for only a few hours each day. Therefore, the connections were not continuous throughout the day. For continuous operation, Hughes Aircraft Company and NASA designed and launched **Syncom 1** into a higher-altitude geosynchronous orbit directly over the ground station in 1963. Although it failed, Syncom 2 and 3, launched later in the year, became the first successful geostationary communications satellites and the basis for later commercial satellites.

The U.S. formed the Communications Satellite Corporation (**Comsat**) in February 1963 as a private company to work with other nations to establish a commercial satellite communications system. In August 1964, Comsat helped create the International Telecommunications Satellite Organization (**Intelsat**) with eleven other countries. Intelsat launched **Early Bird**, the first commercial communications satellite in geosynchronous orbit, on April 6, 1965. Early Bird, also called Intelsat 1, was capable of handling 240 telephone conversations or one television broadcast, and it remained in operation until 1969. Intelsat continued to launch improved satellites throughout the rest of the century. Over 130 member-nations now share ownership and operation of the Intelsat network, which transmits television broadcasts and more than two-thirds of all international telephone calls.

Communications satellites have made live television broadcasts possible to and from anywhere in the world. The advent of satellite broadcasting has helped television become increasingly influential in shaping public opinion. The Vietnam war, for example, became the first "TV war." Every day, viewers could watch news programs in their homes and see the horrors of a faraway war. These images, transmitted by satellite and seen on television, had a major psychological impact on American citizens and spurred their increasingly negative opinions of the war.

The effectiveness of communications satellites have also inspired nations around the world to mutually develop technologies and discover the potentials of outer space. In the process, however, geosynchronous orbit has become overcrowded to the point where interference is a problem.

Because of their advantageous position above the Earth, satellites also proved to be useful for weather forecasting. NASA launched the first weather satellite in April 1960. **TIROS 1** (Television and Infrared Observation Satellite), the first in a series of meteorological satellites of the same name, provided the first photographs of the Earth's cloud cover, and its radiometer measured the radiation caused by heat from the Earth's surface and clouds. TIROS 1 lasted 89 days in orbit and transmitted nearly 23,000 photographs during that time.

Launched in November, **TIROS 2** transmitted more than 20,000 pictures

in 10 weeks, including images of a cyclone in New Zealand and a patch of clouds generating tornadoes in Oklahoma. By spotting these types of dangerous storms, TIROS and other weather satellites became a vital tool in predicting weather to help save lives as well as property. The TIROS series, now in its fifth generation, is still operating and tracking weather from Earth's orbit.

Over the years, satellites have been useful as navigational aids for ships and aircraft, tools for geological and topographic exploration, as well as astronomical and astrophysical research. The military has also employed satellites for many uses, including early-warning detection systems against missile attacks, and for the detection of nuclear explosions in violation of the nuclear test-ban treaty of 1963.

Shedding Light on Lasers

Images of the movie, Star Wars, and of battles fought in the deepest frontiers of outer space are often the first thoughts people have in reaction to the subject of **lasers**. Far from being the death ray of science-fiction lore, however, the laser (Light Amplification by Stimulated Emission of Radiation) is one of the most versatile and useful tools to come out of the 20th century.

Lasers are based on the principle of stimulated emission of radiation, which dates back to a theory introduced by Albert Einstein in 1917. Normal light from sources such as the sun or an electric light bulb radiates in all directions and in different wavelengths. This is called **spontaneous emission**. Einstein stated that under certain conditions,

Townes then joined forces with Canadian physicist **Arthur L. Schawlow** in 1957 and began work on an **"optical maser"** to amplify visible light the same way a maser amplifies microwaves. This proved to be a more complicated and challenging endeavor.

Physicist **Gordon Gould** had similar thoughts. Also in 1957, Gould designed a device he called a laser and wrote the plans in his notebook. He had the notebook notarized, but did not patent it because he mistakenly thought he first needed to build a working model. This mistake led to a legal battle over patent rights that would last for decades.

Townes and Schawlow had a similar idea to make their optical maser work. In a scientific paper published in 1958, they laid out the basic theory and

Arthur Schalow adjusts ruby optical maser

light shining on matter could stimulate the atoms of the matter to emit coherent light of exactly the same wavelength and traveling in the exact same direction as the original light. Scientists accepted the theory of stimulated emission, but initially paid little attention to it because the necessary circumstances for the effect to occur were so unusual.

Applying these principles to microwave radiation, American physicist **Charles H. Townes** invented the **maser** (Microwave Amplification by Stimulated Emission of Radiation) in 1953. In the same way that a laser compresses light into a fine beam, a maser does the same to ultra-short radio waves or microwaves. Masers became useful tools in radio astronomy and in atomic clocks, the world's most accurate timekeeping devices.

Dr. Charles Townes with ruby maser amplifier

ANTI-SHOPLIFTING TAG

Arthur J. Minasy, a consultant for the New York City Police Department, invented the anti-shoplifting tag in his garage in 1964. When attached to store merchandise, the tag set off an alarm as it passed through a security system near the exit. To manufacture and market his invention, Minasy formed the Knogo (pronounced "no go") Corporation.

1959, **Theodore H. Maiman**, a young physicist at Hughes Aircraft Company in Malibu, California, began working on a laser design. Unlike most researchers who were working with gases, Maiman decided to use a solid crystal of synthetic ruby. As his light source, he used a photographer's strobe flash that generated a burst of extremely bright light. The flash bulb was helical — coiled like a spring — and the cylindrical ruby rod was just small enough to fit perfectly between the coils. Maiman then added two parallel silver mirrors, made a small hole in one of them to let the laser beam out, and installed the whole assembly in a reflective aluminum housing. On May 16, 1960, he fired it up, and the contraption released a thin pulse of coherent bright red light.

described a possible design using potassium vapor as an amplifying medium placed between two parallel mirrors. Shining a bright light on it could then bring the potassium atoms to an excited state necessary for stimulated emission. The two physicists patented their design in 1959.

The paper launched a massive effort in the scientific community to develop a laser system based on these principles. In

Maiman had built the first working laser. Within 18 months hundreds of private companies and government agencies had begun their own laser research. Gases and liquids were soon made to "lase." Like Maiman's original device, early lasers generated light only in pulses

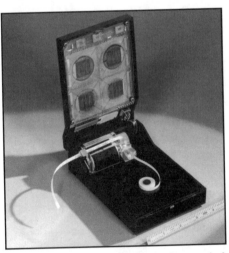

The first electronic hand-held calculator, 1967

or bursts, but in 1961 physicist **Ali Javan** built the first continuous laser, using helium and neon gas.

A laser emits the most intense light beam ever produced, and it travels in an almost perfectly straight line. Unlike normal light, which spreads out as it travels, a laser beam's intensity is hardly affected by distance. When Bell Labs directed a laser beam at the moon in 1962, its light on the moon's surface was only two miles in width and was bright enough to be seen from the Earth. An ordinary light would have spread to about 25,000 miles from the same distance.

Today, lasers are used in countless ways. Almost every industry uses lasers in some form or function. In heavy manufacturing, lasers cut steel with extreme precision and drill materials resistant to other forms of heat. Because they travel in near-perfect lines, lasers are highly accurate measuring tools in surveying and ranging. Surgeons use lasers for delicate eye operations and other procedures, the military uses them for navigation and targeting systems, and supermarkets use them to quickly scan bar codes. The list of applications is vast and constantly growing, but perhaps the laser's most significant use is in communications, especially with the advent of fiber optics in the following decades.

"It was by no means clear, even to those who worked on it, that it would see so many striking applications," Townes later wrote. "And much undoubtedly lies ahead."

Technology and the Environment

Technology may often appear to be miraculously beneficial, but technological advances have led to many unexpected problems. In fact, some technological side effects and byproducts have been shown to be detrimental, and sometimes even outweighs their promised benefits.

In 1962, nature writer **Rachel Carson** published a book, *Silent Spring*, which addressed the environmental impact of technology, especially agricultural pesticides. Carson focused mainly on **DDT**, a pesticide invented in 1939 by Swiss chemist **Paul Müller**. DDT had been considered a marvel of technology because it was so effective at killing insects and significantly increasing crop yields. However, at that time, most people did not realize that DDT also poisoned millions of birds who fed on the contaminated insects. The book's title refers to the lack of bird calls with the coming of spring because of DDT's ill effects upon the bird population.

"Over increasingly large areas of the United States, spring now comes unheralded by the return of the birds, and the early mornings are strangely silent where once they were filled with the beauty of bird song," Carson wrote.

Aside from birds, DDT also killed many beneficial insects and contaminated soil and waterways. Some of the harmful insects, meanwhile, survived the poisoning and developed immunities that they passed down to their offspring. Newer and stronger pesticides then had to be used, and the cycle continued somewhat like an arms race.

Carson raised the question of how to balance our technological needs with the hazards they pose to the environment. Rather than simply focusing on short-term economic benefits, we should also study long-term effects, she said. The underlying theme of *Silent Spring* and the environmental movement that followed is that all life is interrelated and interdependent in a delicate balance.

"Can anyone believe it is possible to lay down such a barrage of poisons on the surface of the Earth without making it unfit for all life?" Carson wrote.

At the time many thought Carson's views were extreme and blown out of proportion. Today, the majority of scientists and environmentalists believe her frightening predictions are to be considered with merit. After being released into the environment, DDT and other pesticides have since been discovered to transform into new forms of poisonous chemicals harmful to wildlife as well as humans. The U.S. banned DDT in 1972 and its derivatives in 1975.

"Our scientific power has outrun our spiritual power. We have guided missiles and misguided men."

Martin Luther King, Jr., Strength to Love

Pollution also became a major environmental issue in the 1960s. As cars became the preferred mode of transportation, their exhaust fumes created a form of air pollution known as **smog** (smoke and fog). Because smog was an especially big problem in Los Angeles, California passed the first state law requiring all cars to install special equipment to limit pollutants from exhaust. Congress then passed the nation's first **Clean Air Act** in 1963, the **Motor Vehicle Air Pollution Control Act** in 1965, and the **Air Quality Act** in 1967.

Indicative of the increased national awareness and concern about the problems of pollution, the President's Science Advisory Committee appointed an

Environmental Pollution Panel in 1965. The panel studied the issues and submitted a report that heavily influenced environmental legislation in the following decades.

"The production of pollutants and an increasing need for pollution management are an inevitable concomitant of a technological society with a high standard of living," the report stated. "Pollution problems will increase in importance as our technology and standard of living continue to grow."

The awareness of adverse technological impacts on the environment and public health would continue to increase throughout the remainder of the century. It is perhaps ironic that the negative side of technology was exposed during the same decade in which some of the most fantastic concepts and ideas of science fiction became reality.

TECHNOLOGY

chapter 8

1970-1979

Information Comes of Age

Floppy disk, 1971

fter the monumental suc-
cess of space exploration
in the 1960s, it appeared
that space would dominate
future technological pursuits. Other
manned flights to the moon followed the
historic Apollo 11 landing in the early
1970s, but tighter budget constraints
quickly made further missions unfeasible.
Since then, manned space flight has been
restricted to within the Earth's orbit. As
it turned out, the peak of human space
exploration came in the same decade as
the first piloted space voyage. The future
of high technology lay not in space, but
in information.

The technological success of landing a
man on the moon was a difficult act to
follow, but the invention of the microprocessor in 1971 contributed to the
dawning of a new era for the industrialized world. The space age was suddenly
eclipsed by the information age. In the
last three decades of the century, information and ways of processing it have
become some of the most important
commodities. Computer technology has
permeated almost every industry and
imposed the need for constantly faster,
smaller, and cheaper equipment to deal
with the exponentially growing quantities
of information on which governments,
businesses, and individuals now depend.

Information is an intangible product,
and is fundamentally different from traditional products of industrial manufacturing. The impact of technological development upon information led to the
development of new forms of businesses
within the service industry. Advances in
technology were coming so quickly that
many people found it difficult to keep up.
Sociologist Alvin Toffler termed the
stressful reaction to such a rapid
onslaught of change "future shock", in his
book with that title, and Daniel Bell

LIQUID CRYSTAL DISPLAY

Efficiency was also increased in
electronic displays with the introduction of the liquid crystal display
(LCD), which uses about 1,000
times less electricity than the
light-emitting diode. Thin layers of
liquid crystals sandwiched
between sections of glass display
groups of individual segments
forming letters, numbers, and even
pictures. Simple LCD systems in
calculators use a seven-segment
format to display numbers, and
more advanced systems later used
in portable televisions, laptop
computers, and hand-held video
games form complex images with
a mosaic of thousands of small liquid crystal cells. Hoffman–La
Roche & Company of Switzerland
patented the first commercial
LCD system in 1971. Unlike an
LED, an LCD does not emit any
light, allowing it to be visible even
in direct sunlight. LCDs, on the
other hand, cannot be seen in the
dark like LEDs. Each display has its
own purpose and both are widely
used.

called the new social structure evolving
to cope with technology the "post-
industrial society".

The most terrifying threat facing the
new society was still nuclear war. With
the nuclear-arms race clearly out of control, the respective leaders of the U.S.
and U.S.S.R., Richard M. Nixon and
Leonid Brezhnev, signed the Strategic
Arms Limitation Treaty (SALT 1) in May
1972. It was the world's first pact limiting production and deployment of
nuclear weapons.

By this time, the U.S. had withdrawn most of its combat troops from Vietnam. Although the nation had not been defeated militarily, the public had grown increasingly disenchanted with the distant war. The lack of progress in subduing a determined enemy, combined with the regular flow of televised carnage, created a psychological defeat in the minds of Americans. In January 1973 the U.S., South Vietnam, North Vietnam, and the Viet Cong signed a cease-fire agreement, and the last American troops left in March. One year later, fighting broke out again. South Vietnam surrendered in April 1975, and became unified with the North into the Socialist Republic of Vietnam. In the process, the U.S. had lost a war for the first time in its history.

On the domestic front, the Nixon administration embroiled itself in the most notorious political scandal in American history. During Nixon's re-election campaign in 1972 a group of men were caught and arrested for breaking into the Democratic Party's national headquarters in the Watergate apartment complex in Washington, D.C. Largely because of Nixon's efforts to cover up the incident, it was not initially linked to him, and he won his second term in a landslide. The ensuing nationally televised investigation and congressional hearings later revealed the attempted cover-up. A series of tape recordings of Nixon's conversations with his aides provided much of the incriminating evidence. In a nationally televised press conference on August 8, 1974, Nixon became the first U.S. president to resign from office. Several other high-ranking White House officials had also resigned by that time. Gerald R. Ford, Spiro Agnew's replacement as vice president, took over the presidency and quickly granted Nixon a full pardon for any crimes he might have committed.

Out of gas sign, 1973

America's dependence on oil as its primary energy source became a liability in October 1973. The Organization of Petroleum Exporting Countries (OPEC) in the Middle East, the main suppliers of the world's oil, banned shipment of petroleum to the United States in retaliation for American support of Israel in the so-called Yom Kippur War earlier that month. The embargo raised gasoline prices by 70 percent in the U.S. and Western Europe and sparked an international energy crisis.

Nuclear power, like power generated from fossil fuels, poses a variety of major drawbacks, including the unsafe disposal of highly toxic waste. A nearly disastrous accident at a Pennsylvania nuclear-power plant, Three Mile Island, reduced the post-industrial society's enthusiasm for fission as a viable source of energy. After the previous decade's advent of satellite communications, the transmission of information through fiber-optic cables, using lasers was the next big advance. Telecommunication is a vital element of the information age, but the computer was and continues to be the era's most prominent technological icon.

Chipping Away

After co-inventing the integrated circuit in 1959, **Robert Noyce** helped turn Fairchild Semiconductor into one of the most successful companies in the booming area south of San Francisco known as **Silicon Valley**. The area was quickly becoming the heart of the world's computer industry. Noyce did not rest on his past achievements, and in 1968, he left Fairchild and started another company called the Intel Corporation.

One of Intel's first jobs was to design a set of 12 integrated circuit chips for a

Intel's Robert Noyce

calculator to be made by the Japanese company Busicom Ltd. While working on the project, former Stanford University physics professor **Marcian "Ted" Hoff Jr**. came up with the idea of incorporating all four basic components of a computer onto a single integrated circuit. The result was a new kind of chip called a **microprocessor**. With a central processing unit (**CPU**), input circuitry, memory, and output circuits all on the microprocessor, the chip could then be programmed for any desired function, just like a normal computer. The "computer on a chip" would soon revolutionize the industry, but Busicom was not impressed.

"When I told the Japanese engineers what I had come up with, they weren't the least bit interested," Hoff said. "They said they were out to design calculators and nothing else."

Despite its client's disinterest in the microprocessor, Intel chose to go ahead and develop Hoff's idea. A prototype was ready in 1970, and Intel introduced the 4004 microprocessor, measuring only 12 square millimeters on November 15, 1971. It was hardly an earth-shattering event. Noyce realized that smaller and cheaper computers were the wave of the future, but other industry leaders could not figure out why anyone would want a small computer. They could not imagine another use for a computer other than its original purpose of manipulating numbers, which is what the term "computing" literally means.

When asked how a microprocessor would be repaired, Hoff explained that it could simply be replaced, much like changing a light bulb. The reasoning sounded absurd, for how could a device as complex as a computer be cheap enough to simply be thrown away and replaced with a new one?

The Altair Computer, 1974

At the time, computer systems were based mainly on mainframe designs, with a large mainframe used for central data processing and numerous terminals allowing other users to access the system. International Business Machines Corporation (IBM) had set the industry standard after it introduced the **System/360** family of computers in 1964. The machines quickly became the most common computers in big business, government, and universities. IBM's dominance drove many companies out of the industry, including corporate giants General Electric and RCA.

Even IBM did not initially fully recognize the microprocessor's significance. The first company to build a small computer utilizing the new and inexpensive chips was Albuquerque, New Mexico-based calculator manufacturer Micro Instrumentation & Telemetry Systems (MITS). The highly competitive calculator market was in the middle of a price war that threatened to put MITS

out of business. Owner **Edward Roberts** was running out of options, and in 1974 he decided to market the first machine now known as a **microcomputer**. Running on Intel's newest microprocessor, the 8080, the **Altair 8800** kit sold for the unprecedented low price of $500. As soon as *Popular Mechanics* magazine introduced the Altair on the cover of its January 1975 issue, Roberts began receiving orders. The Altair was sold unassembled and without a keyboard or screen; it had no software and had to be programmed by manually setting the tiny switches on its front panel. Despite these inconveniences, people bought the Altair, and its sales rescued MITS from probable bankruptcy. More important, it proved that there was a home computer market.

The market initially consisted mainly of computer hobbyists — aficionados obsessed with the new technology. The Altair inspired the formation of several clubs dedicated to computers throughout the nation. The most famous of these was the **Homebrew Computer Club** in the San Francisco area. As the

Steve Jobs and Steve Wozniak with Apple board, 1976

The original Apple board computer

Wozniak in charge of technical design and Jobs taking care of marketing and sales. In 1976 a local retail computer store bought 50 **Apple I** circuit boards and began selling them to the public for $666.66 each.

Wozniak then began designing the **Apple II**, an improved and easier-to-use computer; it was also the first personal computer with color-graphics capabilities and the first to be sold completely assembled.

club grew, some members began forming their own companies to build accessory devices for the Altair, such as additional memory.

Hoping to impress club members, **Stephen Wozniak**, a lifelong Silicon Valley resident, set out to build his own computer. In a matter of weeks he had designed a circuit board with interfaces to connect a keyboard and video monitor. Wozniak showed it to his friend and fellow Homebrew Club member **Steve Jobs**, who suggested the name Apple for the computer.

"I was not designing a computer with any idea that we'd ever start a company, ever have a product, ever be successful," Wozniak said. "It was just to go down to the club and show off, and to own and use."

Jobs, however, had other ideas, and persuaded Wozniak to manufacture and sell the computer. The "two Steves," as they were known, set up shop in Jobs' parents' garage, with

After securing the financial support of local investors, the two Steves moved out of the garage and into a warehouse in nearby Cupertino. At their new headquarters, they continued to work on the Apple II, hoping to make it a computer for everyone, not just computer hobbyists. The Apple II was ready in time to be a hit at the first West Coast Computer Fair in April 1977. By the end of the year, Apple had sold $700,000 worth of computers. Revenues quickly rose to $7 million in 1978.

In view of Apple's success, large and established companies soon entered the personal computer market with their own models aimed at the general public, such as Radio Shack's TRS-80 and Commodore's PET. To remain competitive in the marketplace, Apple needed to offer consumers something unique. At the time, personal computers were using ordinary cassette tapes to store software. Tapes worked, but they were extremely slow and not very dependable. IBM had introduced the floppy disk in 1970, and other

Xerox Mouse

companies were offering disk drives as much faster alternatives to tapes, but they were very expensive and also unreliable. When Apple introduced its floppy disk drive in 1978, it was the cheapest of its kind on the market as well as the best. The Apple II also had a relatively large internal memory, called **random access memory (RAM)**, of 48 kilobytes (48K). More RAM increases the capability to run larger programs at a faster pace.

Apple was heading in the right direction, but a computer's purpose is to run software, and there still weren't many programs available for the personal computer. The company's success was sealed in 1979 with the release of an innovative financial spreadsheet program called **VisiCalc**. As it turned out, the program needed a reliable disk drive and substantial memory to operate effectively. The Apple II quickly became the preferred computer for VisiCalc, and businesses were suddenly buying Apples just to run the program. Other software soon became available, including word processors, graphics programs, educational software, and games. Apple's sales exploded to $48 million in 1979.

Jobs later recalled, "When I saw people that could never possibly design a computer, could never possibly build a hardware kit, could never possibly assemble their own keyboards and monitors, could never even write their own software, using these things, then you knew something very big was going to happen."

Personal computers were obviously making their mark, and in 1980 Apple announced it would become a public corporation and sold its shares in one of the largest offerings at that time. Jobs and Wozniak — still in their twenties — each became instant millionaires, and

VIDEOCASSETTE RECORDER

A common use for **LED** displays is in home videocassette recorders (**VCRs**), because the illumination makes it visible from the couch across the room and in low light. Philips began manufacturing and selling the first home VCR in 1974, but the N1500 was unsuccessful because the half-inch tapes it used ran only for one hour — too short for a feature-length film. VCRs began to become popular only in 1976, when the Japan Victor Company introduced the VHS format for video cassettes, which became the industry standard in the 1980s after a marketing battle with Sony's Betamax system.

Apple Computer became a household name.

As more people began using computers, software developers formed new and successful businesses to provide consumers with programs that would do everything from mundane tasks to entertain. Computers became much more than just machines with which to crunch numbers. Microprocessors, meanwhile, were revolutionizing industries previously unassociated with computers. Acting as special-purpose computers, the tiny chips began to be used to control the operations of a vast array of diverse products, including automobiles, home appliances, and satellites.

Enlightened Communications

The age of information would not be complete without advanced communications systems. As impressive as satellite

Fiber Optics

a straight line, they cannot go around opaque objects in their way, or follow the curvature of the Earth. The only way around these obstacles was to run the laser beams through a special type of wire, just like electrical signals. Called an **optical fiber**, the wire is capable of transmitting light waves. Made of extremely fine, clear glass, the flexible fibers are surrounded by a special coating called **"cladding"** that reflects light back toward the center so it can follow the fiber around twists and turns. This principle is known as **"total internal reflection." Dr. Narinder S. Kapany** of India invented optical fibers in 1955 for use in a device called an **"endoscope"**, which allowed doctors to see around curves inside a patient's body.

In 1966 scientists Charles Kao and George Hockham of England's Standard Telecommunications Laboratories proposed the use of fiber optics as the best medium for the transmittal of communication lasers. Engineers at Corning Glass Works in New York State developed a suitable fiber in 1970, and AT&T's Bell Labs Product Engineering Center in Atlanta had a prototype fiber optics system capable of carrying 50,000 simultaneous telephone calls in 1976. The following year, AT&T installed the world's first commercial fiber-optics cables for an inter-office system in downtown Chicago. On the transmitting end, audio, video, and data are converted into binary code and carried through the fibers on pulses of laser light to the receiver, which converts the digital signals back into their original form. Microchips control the operation of the transmitters and receivers. Further refinements led to the installation of inter-city fiber-optic networks by 1985, and the first transAtlantic fiber-optic cable was installed in 1988.

communications were, the future of telecommunications lay in the field of **fiber optics**.

Like radio and electrical signals, light travels in waves that can carry information. Because light waves have a much higher frequency, they have a higher capacity to hold information. This concept dates back to 1880, when Alexander Graham Bell, the inventor of the telephone, invented a device called the **"photophone"** that used the photoelectric cell selenium to transmit audio signals by sunlight. It was a brilliant idea, but too far ahead of its time to be feasible. Sunlight is too scattered and can be obstructed by clouds, smoke and rain. The photophone also could not be used in the darkness of night.

Eighty years later, in 1960, the laser was invented. It offered new hope for optical transmission, but the problem that still remained was in projecting laser beams to their destinations without running into obstacles. Since lasers travel in

146

Fiber optic cables have many advantages over metallic wire. Because light waves have a higher capacity for information transmittal, one optical fiber, thinner than a human hair, can replace 10,000 telephone wires. Despite their tiny size, the fibers are stronger than steel and more flexible than copper wire, allowing them to curve around tight corners. Optical fibers can transmit an entire encyclopedia in a fraction of a second with unprecedented accuracy. Because they use light rather than electricity, there is no interference or danger of electrocution. The glass used to make optical fibers is refined from silica, or sand, the second most common substance on Earth. It is, therefore, inexpensive, unlike the increasingly rare copper.

Fiber optics is still a young field, yet advances have been rapid and regular. It appears that fiber optics will eventually be the standard transmission medium for telephone service, cable television, and computer interfaces, as well as other communications innovations that may be developed along the way.

ERTS I satellite, 1972

The High Cost of Space Travel

While fiber-optic systems are assimilated into global use, satellites still carry much of the burden for telecommunications. With the launch of **ERTS I** (Earth Resource Technology Satellite) by NASA in 1972, satellites became a useful tool for providing information about various types of activity on the Earth's surface. For example, accurate forecasts of global crop growth and early warnings of crop diseases, detection of forest fires, and the monitoring of water resources became possible as a result of ERTS I. Shortly after its launch, the ERTS I satellite and program were renamed **Landsat**. Several other Landsats have since been put into orbit and some remain in operation today. Circling the Earth 15 times daily at an altitude of 438 miles, Landsat cameras can focus on an area as small as 36 square yards.

> **"You look down there, and you get homesick. You want some sunlight, fresh air, and you want to wander in the woods."**
>
> Cosmonaut Vladislav Volkov from Salyut 1 space station, 1971

The Apollo moon missions continued in the early part of the decade, the first of which almost ended in disaster. Astronauts **James Lovell Jr., John Swiger, Jr.,** and **Fred Haise Jr.** lifted off in **Apollo 13** on April 11, 1970. Their destination was the moon, but an explosion in the Control and Service Module (CSM), nicknamed **"Odyssey"** ruptured an oxygen tank two days into the flight. Approaching the moon, the crew found

Skylab space station, 1973

themselves without air, water, or power in the Odyssey, and moved into the Lunar Module (LM) named **"Aquarius"**, using it much like a lifeboat. In the cramped quarters of the Aquarius, the three astronauts circled the moon and began their voyage back to Earth. Although the LM was designed to accommodate and sustain only two people for 50 hours, the three men managed to survive for 95 hours despite on-board temperatures dropping to near freezing and each crew member consuming only six ounces of water per day. Once they approached Earth, the astronauts re-entered the CSM Odyssey and splashed down in the Pacific Ocean on April 17. An investigation later revealed the cause of the explosion to be a failed thermostatically controlled switch that allowed the oxygen tank to overheat.

Launched on January 31, 1971, the **Apollo 14** mission went more smoothly and achieved a lunar landing. Among the three-man crew was 47-year-old **Alan Shepard**, the first American in space a decade earlier, who also became the oldest person to walk on the moon. Along with Shepard, astronauts **Stuart Roosa** and **Edgar Mitchell** used a mechanized cart to help carry equipment on the surface of the moon. Shepard also brought along a golf-club head, which he attached to a piece of equipment. He used the makeshift golf club to hit two golf balls 200 and 400 yards respectively.

Apollo 15 employed an improved Landing Module to allow more time to be spent on the moon. Landing on July 26 and remaining until August 7, it was also the first mission to use the **Lunar Roving Vehicle** (LRV), also called the "rover." The collapsible vehicle dropped to the moon's surface from the LM and unfolded at the pull of a cord. The four-wheel-drive LRV had enough battery power to cover 55 miles at a top speed of seven miles an hour. Rovers were also used in the 1972 **Apollo 16** and **17** flights, the last piloted moon missions.

"The moon was the metaphor for the unattainable," astronomer Carl Sagan later said. "And look, we had 12 people walking on the surface of the moon. Its historic significance is really hard to overstress."

After the technological challenge of landing humans on the moon was attained, the high cost of such missions, coupled with a tight budget at NASA, made additional flights impractical. While the U.S. was concentrating its efforts on the Apollo program, the U.S.S.R. was developing an Earth-orbiting station. The space station would enable a crew to live and work in orbit for long periods of time. The astronauts aboard the space station would periodically receive fresh supplies and crew sent by visiting craft.

The Soviet Union launched the first space station, **Salyut 1**, on April 19, 1971. The 47-foot-long craft was a series of four cylinders with a diameter of 13 feet at the widest point. Four days later **Soyuz 10** docked with Salyut 1, but the three cosmonauts did not board the space station for unknown reasons and returned to Earth. The station was finally manned on June 6 by the **Soyuz 11** crew. Cosmonauts **Georgi Dobrovolsky, Vladislav Volkov**, and **Viktor Patsayev** stayed on board for three weeks. Unfortunately, on their return, a valve in the spaceship accidentally opened, released their air supply into space, and caused their death by suffocation. By design, Salyut 1 re-entered the atmosphere and burned up after six months in orbit.

Launched in April 1973, the next Soviet space station, **Salyut 2**, could not stabilize in orbit and burned up in the atmosphere the same month. The U.S.S.R. continued to launch Salyut space stations into orbit with greater success. Launched in 1982, **Salyut 7** completed the program when it fell to Earth in 1991.

Two years after Salyut 1 achieved orbit, the U.S. launched **Skylab**, its first and only space station, on May 14, 1973. Three separate crews performed hundreds of experiments on the 118-foot-long Skylab during the Seventies for a total of 171 days. With a two-level workshop about the size of a small house, Skylab prematurely fell back to Earth on July 11, 1979.

As part of the effort to improve political relations between the U.S. and U.S.S.R., the two superpowers embarked on a first-ever collaborative space mission in which an American Apollo and Soviet Soyuz spacecraft were to link up in orbit. The two docking systems were redesigned to be compatible, and on July 15, 1975, **Soyuz 19** took off. Apollo followed about seven hours later, and the ships docked successfully on July 17. The Apollo crew boarded the Soyuz 19 spacecraft and shook hands with the cosmonauts in front of a live Earth-bound television audience. During the two days the spacecraft remained docked, the crews visited one another four times and conducted experiments together. The mission was the last chapter in the Apollo program.

Another endeavor of both space programs was to explore the planets of the solar system. Due to economic and technological limitations, this exploration was accomplished using unmanned probes. NASA launched **Mariner 1**, the first planetary probe, on July 22, 1962, but it went out of control and had to be destroyed shortly after takeoff. The following month, the more successful **Mariner 2** traveled into an orbit around

Pioneer spacecraft set to visit Jupiter, 1972

RUBIK'S CUBE

Setting a VCR clock is often a frustrating puzzle many people would rather avoid, yet an even more frustrating puzzle called Rubik's Cube became an international sensation. Patented in 1977 by Erno Rubik, a Hungarian professor of architectural design, the puzzle consisted of a cube assembled around a sphere, which allowed each of the nine differently colored squares on all six sides to move in every direction. The goal is to position every square of the same color on the same side of the cube, something most people never achieved. After buying the puzzle's manufacturing rights in 1979, the Ideal Toy Company sold more than 100 million Rubik's Cubes worldwide and made $75 million between 1980 and 1983. The success of Rubik's Cube turned its inventor into one of the few millionaires in a Warsaw Pact nation.

the sun, from which it transmitted data for nearly a year. Mars was another subject of interest in which space probes proved useful. Although the Soviet Mars program began in 1962, the only probe to have a successful mission was **Mars 5** in 1973. The American **Mariner 4** flight, meanwhile, completed the first successful Mars exploration when it flew by the "red planet" in July 1965. Launched in May 1971, **Mariner 9** was the first probe to orbit another planet. It spent almost a year in Martian orbit and relayed thousands of images to Earth. **Mariner 10** completed the project in 1974, sending data and images of Venus

and Mercury to Earth. In July 1976, **Viking 1** and **2** took the next step by landing on Mars and transmitting images from its surface.

After two failed flights, the Soviet **Venera 3** crashed onto the surface of Venus on March 1, 1966. Other Venera missions followed, and on December 15, 1970, **Venera 7** became the first man-made object to soft-land on a planet other than Earth and the moon. After 23 minutes of transmission, the probe broke apart due to the extreme temperature and pressure of Venus' atmosphere. Venera flights continued to study Venus until the **Venera 16**, which achieved orbit around the planet in October 1983.

Launched in March 1972, the American **Pioneer 10** became the first spacecraft to fly past the solar system's asteroid belt to explore the outer planets. After spending 10 years studying Jupiter and its moons, Pioneer 10 became the first probe to leave the solar system, in June 1983.

The more advanced Voyager probes explored the outer solar system more thoroughly. **Voyager 2** was launched on August 20, 1977, and **Voyager 1** followed 16 days later. The reversal of order balanced out because Voyager 1 took a more direct route and arrived at Jupiter in March 1979, four months before its counterpart. Among other improvements, the Voyager craft could transmit data 10 times faster than the earlier Pioneer probes. Both Voyagers continued their journeys to the other outer planets: Saturn, Uranus, Neptune and Pluto, in the 1980s, provided valuable information and photographs for earthbound scientists. In the case that either probe came into contact with intelligent extraterrestrial life, each carried a gold-plated copper phonograph record, containing greetings in about 60 languages, and more than an hour of music from various cultures around the world, as well as images of Earth and humans.

Technological Nightmares

Closer to home, Earthlings were still dealing with the age-old problem of reliable and safe energy sources. For the first few decades of the atomic age, nuclear power appeared to be the answer, despite its dangerous radioactive byproducts. Nuclear power plants were coming on-line in the U.S. and around the world. People generally did not feel threatened by nuclear power because there hadn't been any publicized accidents to give them cause for alarm.

> **"The problem of the nuclear power industry is that we have had too few accidents. It's expensive, but that's how you gain experience."**
>
> Sigvard Eklund, general director of the International Atomic Energy Agency, 1980

The situation changed in 1979 when a crisis developed at the **Three Mile Island** (TMI) nuclear power plant near Harrisburg, Pennsylvania. In the early morning of March 28, the water supply used to cool the steam generators was suddenly cut off for unknown reasons, causing the temperature and pressure to soar inside the reactor until safety devices shut it down. A faulty safety valve, however, opened and released thousands of gallons of radioactive water onto the floor of the reactor containment building. The flood triggered the

automatic drainage pumps to turn on and transfer the water into an auxiliary building, where it began to evaporate, releasing radioactive steam into the atmosphere through the ventilation system.

Over the next few days engineers tried to fix the problem, but to make matters worse, a huge hydrogen bubble formed inside the reactor and threatened to explode. As more radioactive steam escaped from the plant, residents began to leave the area. The reactor, owned by the Metropolitan Edison Company, was finally shut down safely and the Nuclear Regulatory Commission officially declared the crisis over on April 9. The disaster was the most serious nuclear accident to date, and it brought the dangers of nuclear power to the forefront of public consciousness. Suddenly the possibility of a meltdown did not seem so far fetched. Public opinion changed so drastically that no new commercial nuclear power plants have been commissioned in the U.S. since the TMI fiasco, and several old ones have been shut down.

The dangers of toxic chemicals were also brought to the public's attention after a tragic episode in the **Love Canal** section of Niagara Falls, New York. The Hooker Chemical & Plastics Company had used an old canal bed in the area as a chemical dump for a period of about 25 years, ending in 1952. After the city took ownership of the land in 1953, a new school and housing tract were constructed on the site. Some time during the next 20 years, the buried chemicals began to leak from their containers, and in the early 1970s children began noticing a thick black substance oozing out of the ground on the school's playground. In 1977, the **Environmental Protection Agency** (EPA) linked the area's abnormally high rates of cancer, birth defects, nervous-system disorders, and miscarriages to toxic-chemical exposure. The state of New York relocated over 200 families in 1978, while the remaining residents were warned about water contamination that might have seeped into their basements and released dangerous fumes in their homes. President Jimmy Carter declared Love Canal a disaster area in 1980, and the remaining residents were relocated at a cost of millions of dollars. In all, over 1,000 families had to be moved from the hazardous area.

Just as the environmental dangers of pesticides were exposed in the previous decade, the impact of other substances also began to be revealed. **Chlorofluorocarbons** (CFCs) had been used for decades as propellants in aerosol cans. Some CFCs help propel the contents of pressure-sealed cans through the release valve. In 1930, **Thomas Midgley** of General Motors, which at the time was the parent company of refrigerator manufacturer Frigidaire, developed **freon**, a type of CFC that is an effective refrigerant used in air conditioners and refrigerators. CFCs were thought to be harmless until a study conducted by scientists **F. Sherwood Rowland** and **Mario José Molino** at the University of California in 1972 proved otherwise. The study found evidence that after CFCs are released into the atmosphere, they break down and contribute to the depletion of the earth's ozone layer, a protective shield against the sun's **ultraviolet** (UV) radiation. Increased levels of UV radiation lead to greater chances of contracting skin cancer, cataracts, and other physical problems for humans, as well as causing numerous detrimental effects to the environment. The United States responded by banning certain CFCs in 1978, and a United Nations agreement

signed by 80 nations in 1989 will phase out CFC production by the year 2000.

Midgley had also discovered that adding lead to a car's gasoline improves engine performance. Lead, however, is a highly toxic substance when burned and released into the air. People became aware of the dangers of lead and other byproducts of a car's exhaust system and caused legislation that made a pollution-reducing device called a **catalytic converter** became standard equipment on American automobiles. When incorporated into an exhaust system, a catalytic converter converts poisonous carbon monoxide and hydrocarbons into harmless carbon dioxide and water vapor. In addition to lead's toxicity, it clogs the reactive surfaces of catalytic converters, making them ineffective. Leaded gasoline, therefore, began to be phased out, and new cars were built to run on unleaded gasoline.

Soaring gasoline prices due to the Middle East oil embargo, meanwhile, caused fuel efficiency to became an important consideration of automotive design. Previously popular large American cars began to be outsold by smaller economy cars made in Japan.

In a shrinking world, it seems appropriate that cars should grow smaller. The quest for miniaturization also became one of the main forces driving the electronics industry and resulted in the invention of the microprocessor. The revolution in computer technology became so widespread that it touched nearly every industry of the modern age.

TECHNOLOGY

chapter 9

1980-1989

The Computer Invasion

NASA's Phantom 2 underwater vehicle uses Virtual Reality

O f all the advances to come out of the century of technology, few have become as dominant as the computer. After decades of performing highly specialized tasks, computers began to gain recognition for their virtually unlimited potential. Once they became accessible to the public in the form of personal computers, software development flourished and programs were created that had mass appeal. Although many people were still uncomfortable working with them in the 1980s, few could deny the rapidly growing impact computers were having.

Personal computers made their way into homes, offices, and schools, and computerized machines became an integral part of industry and daily life. In October 1987 computerized trading facilitated the greatest single-day loss in the history of the New York Stock Exchange. The 508-point drop was even more extreme than the crash of 1929 that started the Great Depression. Thankfully, the result was not as disastrous for the economy.

Under the leadership of President Ronald Reagan, the U.S. experienced the largest peacetime military buildup in its history, which included increases in the number of nuclear and conventional weapons. For the second consecutive decade, an American president was involved in a major scandal as the Iran-Contra fiasco gained national and world attention. In November 1986, the story broke that officials in the Reagan administration had orchestrated a deal to send arms to the anti-American Iranian government in exchange for the release of American hostages. The profit from the sale then went to support the Contra rebels fighting to overthrow the communist government in Nicaragua. Congres-

"To err is human, but to really foul things up requires a computer."

Anonymous

sional legislation had forbidden U.S. assistance to the Contra rebels. Reagan accepted responsibility for his staff's actions, but claimed it was all done without his knowledge or consent.

President George Bush, Reagan's successor, ordered the invasion of Panama in December 1989 to depose the anti-American government of dictator Manuel Noriega, who had also been indicted by a U.S. grand jury on drug charges. American forces quickly captured Noriega and brought him to the U.S. for trial. The invasion marked the first combat missions of the top secret American "stealth" fighter, a high-tech airplane invisible to radar detection.

In the U.S.S.R., Mikhail Gorbachev led the country through an economic and social reform program called "perestroika," or restructuring. A major part of Gorbachev's agenda was the policy of "glasnost," which roughly translates into English as "openness." The goal of glasnost was to give citizens back their voice after being silenced for so long, especially by the repressive and brutal Stalin regime. Gorbachev allowed the Eastern European nations under the Soviet sphere of influence to break free and form independent governments in 1989. On November 9 of that year, the Berlin Wall, the most poignant symbol of Soviet control in Eastern Europe, was opened under pressure from massive protests. Berliners from East and West celebrated the historic event by dancing the night away on top of the wall.

Gorbachev and Reagan signed the

Intermediate-range Nuclear Forces (INF) Treaty in 1987 to eliminate inter-mediate-range nuclear missiles from Europe. The hazards of nuclear power had reared their ugly head again in 1986 when the worst accident in the history of nuclear power occurred at the Soviet power plant at Chernobyl. The explosion of America's newest space vehicle, the space shuttle, occured the same year. Tragically, the Columbia was being used to demon-strate how common space travel could become. The doomed crew included a school teacher, Christa McAuliffe. These two events emphasized the possibility for disaster at even the highest and most respected levels of technological devel-opment.

1981 IBM personal computer

Apart from these tragedies, the com-puter industry continued its growth. After the introduction of the personal computer in the 1970s, the new and eas-ier-to-use operating systems of the 1980s cemented its place as an indis-pensable tool for life in the information age.

Point and Click

Once Apple and other companies found a highly profitable market for per-sonal computers, IBM decided to enter the arena. After dominating the comput-er industry with its highly successful line of mainframe machines, IBM released its first personal computer, the **PC**, on August 12, 1981. The operating system (the software used to run a computer) for the IBM PC was developed by **William "Bill" Gates** and **Paul Allen**, two young computer software entrepre-neurs.

Gates and Allen had proved their technical abilities at an early age. As high

school students in Seattle, the two friends formed a company called Traf-o-Data and developed a system to help control traffic patterns, using an early Intel microprocessor. They sold the sys-tem to the city of Seattle for $20,000 in 1971. Four years later, as students at Harvard University, Gates and Allen spent six weeks writing the operating system for the first personal computer, the Altair 8800. It was a version of a programming language called **BASIC** (Beginner's All-Purpose Symbolic Instruc-tion Code), originally devised by Dart-mouth University mathematics profes-sors **John Kemeny** and **Thomas Kurtz** in 1964. Gates and Allen then formed another company called **Microsoft Corporation** and won the

> **"We call them computers because historically we just happened to use them first for numbers... What they really are is all-purpose machines that can be turned to any purpose by instruct-ing them."**
>
> Ted Nelson, inventor of hypertext

DESKTOP PUBLISHING

In the 1980s computer technology allowed people to perform all the basic functions of creating publications or printed documents with just a few components small enough to fit on a desktop. Whether at home or in an office, anyone with a personal computer, the appropriate software, and a laser printer could generate documents ranging from pamphlets and single-page flyers to magazines and books. The introduction of the desktop laser printer in 1984 made affordable, high-quality printing a reality.

When the attempted 1991 coup by the communist hard-liners in Russia shut down all of the nation's major media, President Boris Yeltsin and his aides used desktop publishing equipment to print an emergency declaration to the Russian people. About 1,000 copies of the document were distributed to alert citizens of the dire situation.

"During the night of August 18 to 19, 1991, the legally elected president of the country was forced from power," the declaration read. "Regardless of the reasons behind this action, we are dealing with a right-wing reactionary, unconstitutional group."

Unlike centralized media, such as newspapers, television, and radio, desktop publishing could occur anywhere, and the coup leaders had no way of stopping it. Word of Yeltsin's publication spread, and the coup fell apart in a matter of days.

Alto computer, created by **PARC** engineers, 1973

contract to develop an operating system for IBM's new line of personal computers in 1980. The result was an innovative new system called **MS-DOS** (Microsoft Disk Operating System) that helped the IBM PC become a monumental commercial success.

In 1983 IBM introduced the fixed hard-disk drive to personal computing with the release of the **PC XT**. Permanently mounted within a computer's body, early hard drives were capable of storing 30 times more data than floppy disks. When turned on, a PC could now **"boot up,"** or activate, its operating system directly from the hard drive rather than requiring the user to insert a series of floppy disks. Within a few years, hard drives became a standard feature on all personal computers, and their memory capacities increased dramatically.

IBM's entry into the personal-computer market did not initially detract from other companies' profits. Quite the contrary was true as sales continued to increase for the entire industry. In 1983, however, sales began to drop. By then, Apple and IBM had emerged as the leading microcomputer manufacturers. That year, they both had just released new computers that flopped: the **Apple III** and the **IBM PC Jr.**, a low-priced version of the PC. In all the excitement about the potential of computers, people began to realize that they were still having trouble using the machines. Users had to learn one or several computer languages to operate personal computers effectively. Computers were just not very "user friendly." Things changed in 1984 with Apple's introduction of a revolutionary operating system in its new personal computer, called the **Macintosh**.

The origins of the Macintosh date back to the early 1970s, before Apple or personal computers even existed. The concept was developed by the Xerox Corporation, the highly successful photocopier manufacturer, which was not previously involved in computer technology. In 1969, Xerox decided to enter the field, and set up the **Palo Alto Research Center** (PARC) in Silicon

Microsoft's Bill Gates

Valley with the objective of making computers easy to use for the average person. The research team decided the best way to achieve this goal was by implementing a graphics-based system, or **graphical user interface** (GUI). At the time, most computers required users to enter an abstract series of codes, which instructed the machines to perform even the most basic operations, such as opening a file. PARC engineers designed a system using graphic icons on the computer screen that would allow users to more readily perform operations.

The keyboard had been the standard method of communicating with a computer, but PARC realized that the best way to interface with a system based on graphical commands was a device called a **"mouse."** Invented by computer engineer **Doug Engelbart** in 1968, its small size and tail-like wire extending from one end made it resemble its rodent namesake. A ball on its underside enabled the mouse to move a corresponding pointer on the computer screen. Using the pointer, one could select objects on the screen (such as files), move them around, or open and close them. PARC used this revolutionary system to create the **Alto** computer in 1973. Xerox, however, did not market

Microsoft Word, 1984

to do. The Alto was an expensive machine, and Apple had to find a way to utilize its high-tech abilities while still maintaining a competitive price in the personal-computer market. Xerox did not have the same vision of affordable personal computing, and released a machine incorporating the Alto system called the **Star** in 1981. It was an excellent computer, but at a price of $16,000 it failed to sell. At the time, most personal computers sold for less than $2,000. Apple, meanwhile, continued to develop an affordable version of the Alto, and on January 23, 1984, the Macintosh hit the market.

the Alto. In the midst of a highly competitive copier market, the company was not willing to take a chance on the Alto. The technology for the computer of the future had to wait.

The future arrived in 1979 when Xerox decided to invest in Apple. As part of the deal, Apple would make and market a computer based on the Alto.

"It was just instantly obvious to anyone that this was the way things should be," Apple co-founder Steve Jobs said after seeing the PARC system.

There was still much work for Apple

The Macintosh was the fulfillment of Apple's original goal with the Apple II in 1977. It was an affordable computer simple enough for even a child to use. The mouse replaced complicated keyboard commands necessary to operate other computers. The screen resembled a familiar desktop. A series of menus offered the user all the possible choices of operations at any given moment. Graphic representations, or **"icons"**, of files were organized into folders. To open something, all the user had to do was position the pointer on the desired icon, click the button on the mouse to select it, and move the pointer to "Open" on the menu. The procedure came to be known as **"point and click."** Once comfortable with the system, users could further simplify the process by just double-clicking on an icon to open it. Moving a file required only dragging its icon with the pointer to another location. The **"drag and drop"** method was also used to move files into the trash icon to be erased. The keyboard was still a useful tool, but it was mostly used to input text into the software rather than for

> **"The establishment does not see where the next wave is coming from. And even if they hire somebody to tell them where the next wave is coming from, they never believe them. Which is exactly what happened with Xerox and Xerox PARC."**
>
> Ted Nelson, inventor of hypertext

commands. By using graphic icons familiar to most people, the Macintosh became the prototypical user-friendly computer in a market full of blank screens waiting for commands few people knew.

IBM's microcomputer was one of those machines, dependent on typed in commands to function. The key to the Macintosh's user-friendliness was not the actual computer hardware; it was the software. Once again, Microsoft provided IBM with a new operating system. Released to the public on November 20, 1985, **Windows** incorporated many of the principles that made the Macintosh successful, including a graphical user interface with mouse-operated commands. Windows, however, was not quite as easy to use as the Macintosh, but millions of IBM users bought the software. It was a big improvement over the previous MS-DOS operating system and was less expensive than Apple. Microsoft continued to release progressively better versions of Windows, but it took another 10 years until **Windows 95** achieved a level of user-friendliness comparable to Apple's Macintosh.

The Evolution of Cyberspace

The personal computer's usefulness and flexibility dramatically increased as people began using it not simply as an isolated machine, but as a means of accessing data on other computers connected to a common network. Several types of computer networks exist today: **Local Area Networks** (LANs) are privately maintained and are usually used within an office environment; several LANs in different geographic locations could be linked as a **Wide Area Network** (WAN). The most far-reaching computer network is the worldwide **Internet**, which is accessible by any computer connected through a channel such as a telephone line with a device called a **"modem."** The Internet has evolved over several decades to become what it is today. Its roots can be traced all the way back to 1957. After the U.S.S.R. launched Sputnik and took the initial lead in the space race, the U.S. Department of Defense (DOD) created the **Advanced Research Projects Agency** (ARPA) to recapture America's status as the world's technological leader. **J.C.R. Licklider**, head of ARPA's computer office, came up with the idea of linking computers so scientists and researchers could efficiently share resources. In 1964, **Paul Baran** of the Rand Corporation think tank in Santa Monica, California, further advanced the idea by suggesting a design for a computer network that could remain an effective communication medium even in the event of a nuclear war. Baran's plan called for a group of interconnected networks forming a larger decentralized network that would remain operational even if one or several portions of the system were destroyed. The surviving parts would redirect communications to their destinations.

Based on these ideas, ARPA set up its computer network in 1969 and named it **ARPANET** (ARPA Network). It originally consisted of four host computers, or **nodes**, located at the University of California at Los Angeles (UCLA), Stanford Research Institute, the University of California at Santa Barbara, and the University of Utah in Salt Lake City. The number of nodes grew to 15 in 1971 and 37 in 1972.

In the meantime, ARPANET users

Stamp commemorating computer technology

In the meantime, ARPANET users began sending each other messages through the network. It was something ARPANET was not initially designed to do, but the system of "electronic mail," or **E-mail**, became one of the network's most useful and commonly used features. E-mail messages were delivered almost instantaneously and consisted of everything from news of the latest breakthroughs to personal gossip. People then began compiling electronic mailing lists that would send the same message to different recipients.

The number of computers connected to ARPANET continued to grow, most of which were still used by researchers. In order for different types of computers to be able to communicate with each other, a language called **Network Control Protocol** (NCP) was introduced in 1973 as a standard for ARPANET connection. An improved system called **Transmission Control Protocol and**

Internet Protocol (TCP/IP) was first used in 1977; it replaced NCP as the standard for connection to ARPANET in 1983.

Also in 1983, the DOD segment of ARPANET broke away and formed its own network called **MILNET** (Military Network), but it was still linked by TCP/IP. The National Science Foundation formed its own network in 1986, called **NSFNET**, that was also connected by TCP/IP. The term **"Internet"** (short for Inter-network) came to signify the rapidly growing conglomeration of separate networks intertwined into one larger network. ARPANET officially ceased to exist in 1990, but few people noticed its absence as the Internet continued to expand and improve. Such was also the case when NSFNET discontinued operation in 1995. True to Paul Baran's vision of an indestructible network, the Internet had grown to incorporate so many fragmented elements that not even a nuclear war, let alone the disintegration of individual networks, could destroy it.

As the number of host computers continued to increase, a system evolved to divide them into **"domains"** depending on their purposes. An Internet address includes one of six types of domain suffixes placed after a unique alphanumerical address: gov (government), edu (education), mil (military), org (non-profit organization), net (network), and com (commercial).

Use spread to individuals as **Internet Service Provider** (ISP) companies began setting up host computers connected to the Internet. Customers could then access the Internet from their own personal computers, with the ISP node acting as a sort of electronic gateway. E-mail remained the most popular feature,

office without the long-distance charges of telephone service. The Internet also has on-line discussion groups called **"newsgroups"** or "USENET." A newsgroup is like an electronic club in which participants exchange information, opinions, and anecdotes about a specific subject. There are thousands of USENET groups on today's Internet, with subjects ranging from nuclear physics and computer science to gardening and basketball. **File transfer protocol** (FTP) allows Internet users to access text and software from other locations on-line. Thousands of Internet "sites" offer free retrieval, or **"downloading,"** of transcribed books, articles, and programs onto a user's own computer. Long-distance computing, the original purpose of ARPANET, remains an important part of the Internet. This allows any computer to become a terminal of other computers, acting somewhat like a remote-control unit. People can use this feature to work on their office computers from their home computers, a practice known as **"telecommuting."** Many libraries have free on-line access to their computerized card-catalog systems, and scientists are able to access distant powerful computers from their portable laptops.

The Internet's vast and intangible world came to be known as **"cyberspace,"** an immeasurable realm of resources available to computer users anywhere on the planet. With new innovations in the 1990s, the Internet's popularity would become astronomical — an appropriate development for the information age.

747-100 with Space Shuttle

New Spaceships

As the new frontier of cyberspace began opening up for exploration, new technologies emerged to help explore the frontier of outer space. The inaugural launch of the American **space shuttle** in 1981 signaled a radical change in space vehicle design. Officially called the **Space Transportation System** (STS), the space shuttle was the first reusable spacecraft.

Four main components comprise the STS: the orbiter spacecraft, two solid rocket boosters (SRBs), and the external tank consisting of fuel, oxidizer, and the three main engines. Resembling an airplane, the orbiter houses the crew and carries payloads to and from space. At lift-off, the orbiter sits upright atop the external tank, which is flanked on both sides by an SRB. The external tank's main engines and the two boosters propel the orbiter into space. The SRBs burn out after two minutes, then separate and fall into the sea for recovery and later reuse. Eight minutes into the flight, the external tank falls away just before the space shuttle achieves orbit; it is the only main component that is not reusable.

Space Shuttle Columbia

an airlock providing astronauts with access to the payload bay and space. Equipment such as air-purification systems and water pumps are located in the lower deck.

President Richard M. Nixon commissioned the space shuttle program in 1972, and the experimental orbiter **Enterprise**, named after the famous spaceship on the "Star Trek" television show, glided to its first landing after being dropped from a modified Boeing 747-100 jet airplane in 1977. The Enterprise completed four other successful Approach and Landing Tests (ALTs) before the STS program was ready for its first space mission, which was scheduled for the orbiter **Columbia** on April 10, 1981. Problems with the computer software, however, delayed the launch for two days. On April 12 the space shuttle Columbia took off from Cape Canaveral, Florida, without incident on its first orbital test flight. Astronauts **John Young** and **Robert Crippen** completed the 54-hour flight and landed safely at Edwards Air Force Base in California.

After completing its mission, the orbiter re-enters the atmosphere, protected from incineration by a vast array of carefully placed tiles, and lands, unaided by engines, on a runway like a glider.

Standing 184 feet tall, the space shuttle has a large payload bay in its center that can carry satellites and other objects to and from orbit. Two massive payload bay doors on its top allow loading and unloading in space, a process made easier by a large mechanical arm called the **Remote Manipulator System** (RMS). The crew compartment at the front of the craft can accommodate eight people comfortably or 10 in an emergency. It is divided into three levels, or decks. The top deck contains the cockpit and workstation with controls for payload bay activity. Day-to-day functions such as sleeping, eating, and storage occur on the mid-deck, which also has

After four more missions by Columbia, the **Challenger** became the second space shuttle to fly into space, on April 4, 1983. On its second flight, launched on June 18, astronaut **Sally Ride** became the first American woman in space. Astronaut **Bruce McCandless** performed the first untethered spacewalk in a **manned maneuvering unit** (MMU) jetpack during a Challenger mission on February 7, 1984. Despite these accomplishments, Challenger will always be remembered for the tragedy of January 28, 1986. Only 73 seconds after taking off in the unseasonably cold Florida weather, the shuttle's external tank exploded, destroying the Challenger and killing its seven-member crew. Among those deceased was **Christa McAuliffe**, a 37-year-old science teacher at Concord High School in New Hampshire. She was to be the first "ordinary citizen" to participate in a space mission and had planned to teach several televised lessons from the orbiting shuttle to children across the United States. The 25th space shuttle mission was the worst disaster in the history of the American space program.

"I know it's hard to understand, but sometimes painful things like this happen," President Ronald Reagan said in a speech on the day of the disaster. "It's all part of the process of exploration and discovery. It's all part of taking a chance and expanding man's horizons."

A presidential commission's investigation found the cause of the explosion to be a faulty O-ring seal, which acts much like a plumbing washer; it allowed flames to leak from the right rocket booster. The air temperature at take off was a major factor in the seal's malfunction; it was colder than it had ever been at any other launch. The disaster forced NASA to suspend the STS program for two years, during which time the O-ring was modified and safety procedures were improved. The three remaining operational space shuttles — **Columbia, Discovery**, and **Atlantis** — were grounded during this period, but the program restarted successfully with the safe launch of Discovery on September 29, 1988. The newest addition to the shuttle fleet, **Endeavor**, embarked on its maiden mission in May 1992.

The Soviet space program, meanwhile, continued on its previous course by launching the space station **Mir** into orbit on February 20, 1986. Similar in size to the Salyut space stations, Mir was designed with separate working and living areas providing a more comfortable environment for up to six cosmonauts, although only two or three are usually on board at a time. The first cosmonauts docked with Mir on March 15, 1986, and it remains the only space station in Earth's orbit. In March 1995, the U.S. and Russia began a cooperative program in which Mir hosts a series of American astronauts arriving and departing by space shuttle. The shuttle is also used to deliver supplies along with passengers. As the Cold War also came to an end, and the competitive nature of the space race ceased, space exploration became more cooperative.

Catastrophes Continue

The Cold War was still active, however, in the early 1980s, and nuclear-weapon arsenals continued to grow larger. Nuclear war was already a terrifying concept, but a new theory claimed that its aftermath would be far more grave than previously imagined. In 1983 a group of scientists, including the famous astronomer **Carl Sagan**, introduced the idea of **"nuclear winter"**, a condition that would be caused by a worldwide nuclear war. A large-scale nuclear exchange would raise enough dust and smoke to block sunlight from reaching the surface of the Earth for possibly an entire year. Temperatures would subsequently fall to levels below freezing, and plants would be incapable of carrying out photosynthesis, the process, essential to life, of converting carbon dioxide into oxygen with the help of sunlight. As a result, most organisms, including humans, would die, and when the dust finally cleared, a depleted ozone layer would allow high levels of solar radiation to blind any survivors.

The B-2 Stealth Bomber

"It is... entirely possible that the biological impacts of a (nuclear) war, apart from those resulting directly from a blast, fire, and prompt radiation, could result in the end of civilization in the Northern Hemisphere," **Paul Ehrlich** wrote in *The Cold and the Dark: The World After Nuclear War.* "Biologists can agree to that as easily as we all could agree that accidentally using cyanide instead of salt in the gravy could spoil a dinner party."

Hopefully, the theory of nuclear winter will never be tested. A test at a Soviet nuclear power plant, however, became the worst nuclear accident in history. On April 25, 1986, managers of the **Chernobyl** nuclear-power station in the Soviet Ukraine ordered an experiment to see how long the reactor could pro-

duce power after shutting down. The ill-fated exercise quickly became too much for the plant operators to handle, and they proceeded to make a series of mistakes that disengaged several backup safety systems. In the early hours of the following morning, the reactor overheated and set off a series of explosions. Within half an hour, the thousand-ton concrete lid of the containment vessel was blown through the roof, releasing a massive radioactive cloud into the sky. The wind carried dangerous amounts of radiation across the Ukraine and into Europe.

The U.S.S.R. did not announce the disaster until a Swedish nuclear power plant detected radiation levels 20 percent higher than normal two days later. The reactor at Chernobyl was still burning out of control at this time, and no one was sure how to stop it. More than 100,000 residents within a 19-mile radius were evacuated as helicopters dropped sand and concrete onto the reactor in an attempt to smother the fire. The reactor burned for nine days; it was eventually sealed in a concrete tomb.

Thirty-one people, mostly plant workers, died shortly after the accident and 500 were hospitalized, but the longer-term effects of radiation exposure were far more devastating. The death toll as a result of Chernobyl is now estimated at more than 125,000 and growing as people continue to die from radiation-related diseases such as cancer. The radiation also caused widespread birth defects in humans and animals. The radioactivity in the vicinity of Chernobyl is expected to remain at dangerous levels for at least another century. Despite the unsafe environment, many of the local residents have returned to the evacuated area.

Cleanup efforts have cost billions of dollars.

The 1980s had an unusually high share of industrial accidents, and one of the worst was at an American company's pesticide plant near the central Indian city of **Bhopal**. Shortly after midnight on December 3, 1984, a storage tank at the Union Carbide factory began leaking toxic gas into the air of Bhopal. The deadly cloud soon covered the city, killing people in their sleep, while others woke up vomiting and feeling that their lungs were burning. The streets quickly became filled with people and animals desperately running for safety, many of whom fell dead. The plant's alarm did not go off for two hours, by which time the carnage could not be stopped. About 2,000 people died that night, but like nuclear radiation, the toxic gas of Bhopal had lingering effects. Thousands more died over the years and about 200,000 were left with various injuries and afflictions. In 1989 India's Supreme Court ordered Union Carbide to pay $470 million in damages.

The worst oil spill in American history occurred on March 24, 1989, when the oil tanker **Exxon Valdez** ran into a reef in Alaska's Prince William Sound. The ship's ruptured hull released 11 million gallons of crude petroleum and caused severe ecological damage. After substantial public outcry, Exxon attempted to clean up the mess and fired the ship's captain for drinking while on duty.

Space Age Technology
▬ ▬ ▬ ▬ ▬ ▬ ▬ ▬

In 1989, the U.S. Air Force's new **stealth** technology, which enabled an aircraft to fly without being detected by radar, saw its first combat action during the American invasion of Panama. Secretly tested throughout the 1980s, the **F117A** stealth fighter/bomber (nicknamed the Wobbly Goblin) used a special coating and unconventional angles to absorb radar waves rather than reflect them. The **B-2** stealth bomber, unveiled in 1988, uses a similar coating, but unlike the Wobbly Goblin's sharp angles, it has a smoothly shaped exterior. The B-2's unique "flying wing" design disperses its weight in a triangular configuration.

Despite the futuristic appearance of these stealth aircraft, they do not fire laser guns. Lasers, however, found a new and peaceful use in 1982 with the introduction of the **compact disc** (CD) as a result of a joint effort by two electronics companies; Philips and Sony. A CD is a 4.7-inch plastic disc on which digital audio signals are stored and read back by a laser beam. Unlike an analog record, a CD stores its signals in binary code burned into the disc's surface as a series of microscopic pits. The pits are assigned a binary value of one, and the smooth areas, or land, are read as zeroes. A laser beam scans the binary coded signals as the CD spins and converts them back into an audible sound to be heard through the stereo system's loudspeakers.

CD technology eliminated all background noise common on vinyl records caused by imperfections such as scratches and dust in the grooves. The lifespan of a CD is much longer than a conventional vinyl record, since the laser beam does not cause wear on the disc with repeated use.

CDs were also applied to the storage of computer data in the form of **CD-ROM** (Compact Disc Read-Only Memory). Their incredible storage capacity has made them useful for prepackaged software such as computerized encyclopedias, but unlike hard drives and floppy disks, CD-ROMs are manufactured with encoded data that cannot be erased, and no additional data can be written onto them.

Cell phone

Mobile communications took a big step forward in 1983 with a new **cellular system** regulating portable telephones, which use radio waves to transmit and receive audio signals. Before this time, mobile telephone service in the U.S., consisting mainly of car phones, was extremely limited because metropolitan areas had only one antenna for these purposes. In addition, the Federal Communications Commission (FCC) assigned only 12 to 24 frequencies to each area, meaning that only that many calls could occur at a time. These limitations often meant a wait of up to 30 minutes for a dial tone and a five to 10

year waiting list just to acquire the service.

With the introduction of the cellular system in 1983, urban areas were divided into zones, or **cells**, each with its own antenna. The size of the cell depended on the number of users within it, and cells could be further divided as usership increased. The FCC issued its cellular-telephone requirements in 1981, and Ameritech Mobile Communications launched the first American commercial cellular service in Chicago in October 1983.

With the arrival of cellular phone service, personal communications broke free of wires. In the 1990s it would become possible to connect to the Internet from virtually anywhere in the world, using a portable computer and a cellular modem with satellite service. Technologies developed from seemingly different fields, such as personal communications, computation, and space exploration, often worked together to serve the constantly evolving human needs of the information age.

TECHNOLOGY

chapter 10

1990-1999

Riding the Information Superhighway to a New Millenium

Enlarged microchip

The age of information reached new heights in the final decade of the 20th century. Personal computers became a common fixture in both businesses and homes, and their usefulness increased with the explosive popularity of the Internet. Following in the technological footsteps of the printing press, the telephone, radio, and television, the Internet established itself as the next great tool for mass communication. Like its predecessors, the Internet drastically improved the transmission of information and ideas to different parts of the world. The perception of a shrinking world was more vivid than ever before.

A new development in the 1990s called the World Wide Web (WWW) helped bring the Internet into the main-stream after years of being a tool used primarily by researchers and programmers. During the 1992 U.S. presidential campaign, Democratic nominee Bill Clinton and running mate Al Gore focused heavily on the establishment of an "information superhighway," which would incorporate the Internet and other media such as television and publishing, linked by an extensive network of fiber optic cables. Clinton and Gore won the election, the information superhighway took off, and the sudden popularity of the Internet made the once "nerdy" subject of computers fashionable.

As the world was shrinking, it was also changing. In February 1990 the Soviet Communist Party gave up control after more than 70 years of domination. The following month, Lithuania declared its independence, and the U.S.S.R. was on its way to disintegration. Other Soviet provinces, or republics, followed, and Boris Yeltsin became the first freely elected president of the new Russian Republic in June 1991. Loyal Communist Party members refused to stand idle and watch the Soviet Union crumble. In August they attempted a coup, but it failed within a few days, and the Communist Party was subsequently outlawed. The leaders of the eleven republics officially ended the Soviet Union's existence in December and created a loose coalition called the Commonwealth of Independent States.

The Cold War had ended by the beginning of the decade, and the balance of power in world affairs shifted heavily in favor of the U.S. However, it wasn't long before America was at war again,

Middle East refinery

OPTICAL COMPUTER
■ ■ ■ ■ ■ ■ ■ ■ ■ ■

In January 1993 electrical engineers Vincent Hueing and Harry Jordan at the University of Colorado built the world's first fully optical computer, which uses light traveling through optical fibers to store and process data. To make conventional computers faster, manufacturers use the smallest microchips possible to minimize the distance electrons have to travel. There is a limit, however, to how small chips can get once the molecular level is reached. Smaller chips also have the problem of radiation interference when the tiny wires are so close together. Optical computers are not limited by these factors, because light has no mass or electrical charge; it also travels at the fastest possible speed. Hueing and Jordan's optical computer was only a prototype incapable of performing complex calculations, due to limited memory, but its intention was simply to prove that such a machine can function — a goal it fulfilled.

this time in the Middle East. Under the leadership of dictator Saddam Hussein, Iraq invaded neighboring Kuwait, an important oil-producing nation, in August 1990. The United Nations condemned the Iraqi invasion and threatened to retaliate if Hussein did not remove his troops by January 15, 1991. Hussein did not comply, and the U.N. offensive, carried out mostly by the U.S. and known as Operation Desert Storm, began with the bombing of Iraq the day after the deadline. The ground invasion began in February and Kuwait was liberated with-

in 100 hours. The defeated Iraqis released 168 million gallons of crude oil into the Persian Gulf, causing history's largest oil spill. Iraqi soldiers also set fire to 730 Kuwaiti oil wells, resulting in an inferno that burned for nine months.

The Persian Gulf War was the latest incident to highlight the problems of a society heavily dependent on oil, a limited resource with much of it coming from the turbulent Middle East. Society has long searched for a suitable alternative to petroleum but has been unable to replace it as the principal energy source. Recent advances in a device called a "fuel cell," however, indicates that automobiles may no longer be running on gasoline. In the future, scientists hope to harness nuclear fusion, the same process behind the hydrogen bomb, into a safe and efficient power source. Scientists working with superconductors, meanwhile, hope to provide a highly efficient transmission system for electricity.

While the future may look bright for alternative energy sources, the hottest technology of the 1990s remains the Internet, and especially the World Wide Web, also known simply as "The Web."

Weaving a Web
■ ■ ■ ■ ■ ■ ■ ■ ■ ■

The impact of the **World Wide Web** on the Internet can be compared to that of the Graphical User Interface (GUI) on personal computers; developed by Xerox PARC and incorporated in the Apple Macintosh (and later in Microsoft Windows), the GUI made personal computers easier to operate by allowing users to simply point and click to perform any function. This revolution of user-friendliness, however, did not affect the Internet until the introduction of the Web, which made the Net easier to operate and navigate.

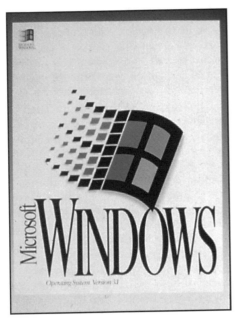

1992 Windows version 3.1

The World Wide Web was invented in 1989 by British computer specialist **Tim Berners-Lee** at **CERN** (Counseil Européen pour la Récherche Nucléaire, or the European Laboratory for Particle Physics) in Geneva, Switzerland. Berners-Lee's purpose was to create a system through which the world's high-energy physics researchers could collaborate and share information over long distances using **"hypertext."** Developed

"It's like the difference between the brain and the mind. Explore the Internet and you find cables and computers. Explore the Web and you find information."

Tim Berners-Lee, World Wide Web inventor

by **Ted Nelson** in 1960, hypertext allows the user to access more information on a given subject by clicking on highlighted keywords (often underlined) and images with a mouse pointer. Clicking on these **"links"** retrieves the requested data and displays it on the computer screen. Berners-Lee applied hypertext to the Internet and made navigation a simple matter of pointing and clicking.

"I realized that if everyone had the same information as me, my life would be easier," Berners-Lee said.

After several test versions of the Web were put into use within the physics community, CERN released it to the public in May 1992. The World Wide Web is based on a **"client-server"** model in which a program (the client) allows the user to retrieve data from a remote host computer (the server). The system introduced by CERN worked, but a user-friendly client, or Web **"browser,"** compatible with PCs and Apples did not yet exist. Berners-Lee's browser worked only with a computer

Jim Clark from Netscape

called **NExT**, which was rarely used out-side scientific circles, and the Web remained an obscure phenomenon.

The scenario changed in February 1993 when **Marc Andreessen** and a group of fellow students at the University of Illinois' **National Center for Supercomputing Applications** released a browser called **Mosaic** that was compatible with both the PC and Macintosh. Mosaic made it possible for users of these different operating systems, or **"platforms,"** to interconnect and exchange information. It was also an easy-to-use program capable not only of displaying text and graphics, but also playing computerized movies, audio tracks, and just about anything else. Mosaic unleashed the World Wide Web's multimedia potential.

Further simplifying the Web, Mosaic's programming was based on an easy-to-learn computer language called **HTML** (Hypertext Mark-up Language). Using HTML, anyone could set up his or her own site, or information page on the Web. These sites, requiring a modem and telephone line to access, are located on-line at a sort of electronic address called a **URL** (Universal Resource Locator). Andreessen and his colleagues distributed Mosaic free on the Internet, and its popularity, as well as that of the World Wide Web, began to spread at an explosive rate. The number of people using the Web in 1993 was 3,000 times greater than in 1992. For many people, the World Wide Web became synonymous with the Internet.

Mosaic's impact on popularizing the World Wide Web led to its label as the Internet's first **"killer application,"** an application program so revolutionary that it could spawn a brand-new industry singlehanded. Mosaic opened up a whole new avenue for commerce. It suddenly

Marc Andreessen from Netscape

became possible to buy and sell goods on the Web, as well as advertise.

One person who recognized the commercial value of this killer application was **Jim Clark**, then chairman of Silicon Graphics, a high-end computer company he founded in 1982. Clark left Silicon Graphics in February 1994 and contacted Andreessen by E-mail with an invitation to start a new company with him. Andreessen agreed, and in April 1994 Netscape Communications Corporation was born. Netscape's mission was to turn Mosaic into a commercial product and become the world's primary Internet software company. To help achieve these goals, Clark and Andreessen hired five of the remaining six original Mosaic developers from NCSA. After a few months of grueling work in its Silicon Valley headquarters, the Netscape team completed the first version of its Mosaic browser, called **Navigator**.

With the software complete, the next step to industry domination was to quickly get the program onto as many computers as possible. Andreessen proposed the same strategy he used with the original Mosaic — give away free

FLASH MEMORY CHIPS

▬ ▬ ▬ ▬ ▬ ▬ ▬ ▬ ▬

Reminiscent of the microprocessor, which put a computer on a chip, flash memory chips do the same for hard drives. In 1992 Intel introduced a chip that stores long-term memory and is smaller, faster, and more energy-efficient than a hard drive. Because the plug-in flash memory card does not have any moving parts, it is also incapable of "crashing," or mechanically malfunctioning and rendering the computer inoperable. Flash memory, however, is still expensive, but its price is expected to drop until it can eventually compete commercially with hard drives.

Flash memory chips (Intel)

trial copies on the Web. The idea initially sounded crazy to other executives, but Andreessen had his way, and on October 14, 1994, Netscape made the first test versions of Navigator available on-line.

The strategy worked. By spring 1995 six million copies of the browser had been downloaded, and when Netscape's stock went public on August 9 it became one of the hottest initial public offerings in Wall Street history. Sales increased in 1996 by 305 percent. In two years Netscape distributed 50 million copies of Navigator, and it became the world's second most common program, behind Microsoft Windows.

New versions of Navigator have additional functions that allow it to be used for Internet purposes other than "surfing" the Web. Netscape has made its browser more flexible by adding built-in features to handle capabilities that previously required separate programs

for each, such as electronic mail, file transfer protocol (FTP), and newsgroups.

Netscape continues to offer free trial versions of the latest Navigator software on-line, but more than half of its revenues come from browser sales. Netscape also generates revenues through advertising, and Navigator is the world's most common browser. The Netscape home page is one of the busiest on the Web, making it a favorite with advertisers. As with television stations and magazines, companies can sell advertising space on their Web sites. The number of people accessing a site can be tracked relatively accurately by recording the number of "**hits,**" or visits.

Netscape's dominance in the World Wide Web market, however, is being challenged by the giant Microsoft Corporation, which released its first Web browser, **Internet Explorer**, in August 1995. Microsoft, using its massive corporate resources, made a conscious decision to attempt to take over the market from the upstart Netscape.

"The Internet is the most important

thing going on for us," Microsoft chairman Bill Gates said. "It's driving everything at Microsoft."

Thus the great corporate technological rivalry of the 1990s was established, and the battle for Internet supremacy continues to be fought as the end of the century approaches.

New Trains: Underwater and in the Air

Although they have a long history as rivals, France and England joined together to build a subterranean tunnel beneath the English Channel and connect the two nations by railway. The resulting **Channel Tunnel**, also called the **"Chunnel,"** has been called the greatest engineering accomplishment of the century.

The idea for a tunnel beneath the English Channel is an old one. In 1802 French mining engineer **Albert Mathieu-Favier** first conceived a plan for such a tunnel. Since the railroad locomotive had not yet been invented, the proposed tunnel was intended for stagecoach travel. The design called for a series of chimneys reaching above the water's surface to provide ventilation for the tunnel. French ruler Napoleon Bonaparte liked the concept, and although there was a truce between England and France at the time, the British did not think it was a good idea to give the militant Napoleon a convenient avenue of attack. The plan was also impractical, and construction was never attempted. Several other plans for building a tunnel were attempted over the years, but none were successful. Insufficient technology and poor relations between the two countries made such a massive project

impossible until the latter part of the 20th century. Great Britain and France signed the Channel Tunnel Treaty in February 1986, and companies from both nations participated in the construction, which began the following year.

Boring through the ground beneath one of the most turbulent waterways in the world was a daunting task. It was facilitated with special equipment built especially for the undertaking, including the world's largest drill, capable of cutting through 2,000 tons of rock per hour. Starting from opposite sides of the Channel, the British and French crews worked underground for three years before meeting in the middle.

Linking Folkestone, England, with Calais, France, the Chunnel runs a total of 31 miles, with 23 of the miles beneath the channel. The Channel Tunnel actually consists of three tunnels — one for northbound train traffic, one for southbound traffic, and one in between for service and repairs. More than 17 million tons of earth were displaced to build the tunnel. The rubble added 90 acres of land to England; the extra area was used for a new park.

The Chunnel was finally completed in 1994 at a cost of $15 billion, and on May 6, Queen **Elizabeth II** of England and French President **François Mitterrand** embarked on the inaugural channel crossing of the brand-new, state-of-the-art **Eurostar** train. Eurostar service connects London with both Paris and Brussels and can comfortably transport 794 passengers — in trains traveling at 80 miles an hour through the Chunnel and up to 186 miles an hour once in France. The trip from London to Paris takes three hours, and London to Brussels takes three hours and fifteen minutes. The actual tunnel crossing time is just 21 minutes.

Apart from the advantage of increased speed, maglev trains also require less maintenance because the lack of friction practically eliminates the mechanical wear and tear on the track and the train's suspension system. The magnets' polarity not only levitates the train off the track, but also propels it with electromagnetic waves, a system known as a **"linear synchronous motor"** (LSM). The train, in effect, rides these magnetic waves much like a surfer rides waves in the ocean. Slowing the train down is simply a matter of reversing the direction of the waves. The frictionless design is more energy efficient as well as quieter than conventional trains.

The Meisner Effect

The Eurostar is one of the fastest conventional trains in the world, but like most locomotives, its speed is limited by the friction of the wheels against the track. A radically different approach to railway design has eliminated friction by using the repulsive forces of magnets to elevate trains over their tracks so there is no contact between the two surfaces. These magnetically levitated (**maglev**) trains have already been constructed as prototypes, and Germany is currently building a commercial maglev line between Hamburg and Berlin. The first section of the 175-mile railway is scheduled to open for operation in 1998, with complete inter-city service beginning in 2005. Prototypes of the German maglev train, called the **Transrapid**, have achieved speeds of up to 290 miles an hour while elevated one-half inch above the track.

The Magic of Superconductors

While the German maglev train employs ordinary magnets, another alternative for levitation is the use of materials called **"superconductors."** When electricity travels through normal conductive materials (usually metals such as copper), part of the current is lost to the conductor's resistance, which is similar to friction. In 1911 Dutch physicist **Heike K. Onnes** discovered that when the metal mercury is cooled to an extremely low temperature its electrical resistance is eliminated, making it a highly efficient conductor of electricity, or superconductor. Onnes had to lower the mercury's temperature to 4 Kelvin (-454° Fahrenheit), which is just slightly above the absolute lowest possible temperature (0 Kelvin, or absolute zero, is equal to −460° F). It was an important discovery, but such extremely low temperatures are difficult and expensive to achieve, and few applications for superconductors were practical.

Over the next several decades, scientists attempted to find superconductive materials that work at higher and more manageable temperatures, but the increases were minor. Many scientists subsequently gave up the quest for a high-temperature superconductor. In January 1986, however, Swiss physicist **K. Alex Müller** and his German colleague **J. Georg Bednorz** at IBM's Zurich Research Laboratory in Switzerland made the important discovery that certain ceramics become superconductive at much higher temperatures than metals. They created a ceramic compound capable of superconducting at 35 Kelvin (−396° F), a dramatic improvement over the previous high of 23 Kelvin (−418° F) achieved in 1973. An entirely new class of superconductors was born, called **high-temperature superconductors** (HTS); the earlier metallic superconductors are known as **low-temperature superconductors** (LTS).

The scientific world was captivated by the news, and the race was on for ceramics that superconduct at higher temperatures. It wasn't long before the next great discovery. On January 28, 1987, Chinese-born physicist **Paul Ching-Wu Chu** of the University of Houston and colleague **Maw-Kuen Wu** at the University of Alabama synthesized a ceramic that was superconductive at an incredible 93 Kelvin (−292° F). This tremendous increase in the required temperature meant superconductivity could now be achieved by using liquid nitrogen for cooling, which is much less expensive than the liquid helium

necessary to cool an LTS.

"We were so excited and so nervous that our hands were shaking," Wu said of the successful experiment. "At first we were suspicious that it was an error."

Within a few days, Chu and Wu had raised the temperature to 98 Kelvin (−283° F). Since then, superconductors have been discovered at temperatures as high as 130 Kelvin (−225° F). Scientists are still searching for materials with superconductive properties at room temperature.

"Nobody ever thought ceramics would do this," Donna Fitzpatrick of the U.S. Department of Energy said soon after Chu and Wu's discovery. "Why should a ceramic conduct? That was the most interesting part of the whole thing."

Superconductors are of great interest to electrical companies because they are much more efficient than standard conductors. An estimated 15 percent of electricity generated today is lost to resistance when transmitted through metallic wires. The next problem to be solved is how to manipulate superconductive ceramic material into wires. It is a difficult task, for ceramic is very brittle and inflexible, unlike more traditional conductors.

"(It is like) turning a coffee cup into a wire," IBM researcher Paul Grant explained.

Superconductors also display a characteristic known as the **Meissner effect**. Discovered in 1933 by German physicists **Walther Meissner** and **Robert Ochsenfeld**, the Meissner effect is a superconductor's ability to repel magnets regardless of their polarity. In other words, a magnet placed over a superconductor will float in the air. This property is what makes for lighter trains, higher possible speeds, and more space between the vehicle and the track; the Japanese trains can fly up to six inches above the guideway and are less susceptible to potential problems caused by poor weather.

"It's not a locomotive technology, really, but an aerospace one," said Larry Johnson of Argonne National Laboratory's Center for Transportation Research in Illinois. "What you have here is a 300-mile-an-hour levitated fuselage, and the principles behind that are those of an aircraft."

A new Japanese test line for superconducting maglev trains was scheduled to open in the spring of 1997, and a decision is expected to be made on the system's commercial future after three years of testing at the new facility.

Replica of the Hubble Telescope

superconductor-based maglev trains possible.

American engineers **James Powell** and **Gordon Danby** came up with the idea for a superconducting magnetically levitated train and published their ideas in 1966. They received the first patent for a maglev system in 1968. Fascinating as the concept appeared, it did not attract much attention, but the Japanese decided to develop the system and had a working model on exhibit at the 1970 Osaka World's Fair. A test-run of a Japanese maglev train set a world record in 1979 with a speed of 321 miles an hour. The advent of ceramic superconductors simplifies the cooling process, but it is still a more complex and expensive technology than the German maglev system. Superconductors, however, allow

International Space

Scientists speculate that superconductors may someday be capable of launching spaceships from vertical electromagnetic tunnels. For the present time, the rocket-powered space shuttle is still the world's most advanced spacecraft. Launched on April 25, 1990, the space shuttle **Discovery** deployed one of the most anticipated and beneficial tools for space research — the **Hubble Space Telescope** (HST).

Named for **Edwin Hubble**, the American astronomer who in the 1920s postulated the theory of a constantly expanding universe, the HST was launched as a cooperative effort of NASA and the **European Space Agency** (ESA). The billion-dollar telescope was designed to allow scientists to see deeper into space than was ever possible with previous earthbound equipment, but the images it transmitted to astronomers on Earth were blurry. As it turned out, the HST's eight-foot primary mirror was improperly curved. Although the flaw was smaller than the width of a human hair, it was serious enough to blur images and render the telescope practically useless. The HST needed to be fixed, and the only way to do it was to perform the repairs in space.

Seven astronauts trained rigorously for 10 months, simulating weightlessness in large underwater tanks and working in a cold chamber with space-like temperatures of 300 degrees below zero. On December 2, 1993, the astronauts took off aboard the space shuttle **Endeavor** to repair the 12.5-ton orbiting telescope. After harnessing the HST into the shuttle's cargo bay and completing a record of five spacewalks, the crew installed corrective optics as well as a new camera. Endeavor released the telescope back into orbit on December 10. Images received from the HST on December 18 confirmed that the complicated mission was a resounding success.

On February 3, 1994, the space shuttle Discovery launched a small orbiting laboratory called the **Wake Shield Facility** (WSF) into orbit. Designed and built by the Space Vacuum Epitaxy Center at the University of Houston and Space Industries Incorporated, the 12-foot-diameter stainless-steel disk utilizes the vacuum of space to minimize contamination in the production of **gallium arsenide**, a semiconductor with the potential to be used in microchips 10 times faster than those made of silicon. A vacuum is a space devoid of matter — an ideal condition for the production of semiconductor crystals because it contains no particles to contaminate the process. Taking advantage of the space

environment, which is thousands of times more sterile than any vacuum created on Earth, the WSF conducted a series of thin- film growths, a process called **"epitaxy,"** to produce extremely pure crystals of gallium arsenide. After completing this procedure, the space shuttle returned the laboratory back to Earth on February 11. Other WSF missions were launched in September 1995 and November 1996, and one more is scheduled to be completed before the end of the century.

If plans go smoothly, an effort by space agencies of numerous nations will place an international space station into orbit shortly after the turn of the century. NASA is teaming up with the European Space Station, the Russian Space Agency, the National Space Development Agency of Japan, the Canadian Space Agency, and the Italian Space Agency. A total of 14 nations are cooperating to build and launch the **International Space Station**. The target date for completion is 2002, with the launching of the first components scheduled for November 1997.

New and Improved Energy

One of the technological spinoffs of space exploration has been the **fuel cell**, an efficient energy-producing device that causes no pollution. By combining oxygen from the air with the element, hydrogen, in a chemical reaction, a fuel cell generates electricity and heat without burning fuel, or moving parts, unlike the internal combustion engine used in conventional automobiles. Because the only elements involved in the process are hydrogen and oxygen, the only substance emitted is pure, drinkable water.

The fuel cell was invented in 1839 by British scientist **William Grove**, but the early models generated only a small amount of electricity, and the device remained widely ignored until NASA decided to use an improved version, beginning with the Gemini 5 mission on August 21, 1965. The fuel cell generated power for the spacecraft, and the water it produced as a byproduct helped keep the astronauts from dehydrating. Fuel cells also provided power and water on the Apollo missions, and NASA still uses them on its space shuttle flights.

In the early 1980s, Japanese interest in fuel-cell technology began to intensify. Several fuel-cell power plants have been constructed in Japan since that time, and tests have shown considerable promise. A prototype unit produces electricity and heat for the Plaza Hotel in Osaka. The first commercial fuel cell in the U.S. was installed on May 22, 1992, at the headquarters of the **South Coast Air Quality Management District** (**SCAQMD**), an air-pollution control agency in Southern California, an area with the worst air quality in the U.S. Fuel-cell generators are now in operation at a handful of locations within SCAQMD's jurisdiction.

Studies have shown that 70 to 80 percent of the air pollution in the Los Angeles area is a result of automobile emissions. Recent advances indicate that fuel cells will likely power cars of the future, which would run on electricity. Unlike other electric cars that have been proposed over the years, a fuel-cell powered vehicle does not need to be recharged, but simply refueled with hydrogen. The recharging of battery-powered cars causes more pollution than those that run on fuel cells because power plants need to burn more fossil fuel to provide electricity for these vehicles.

Using fuel cells, a Canadian company, Ballard Power Systems, completed construction of the world's first **zero-emission bus** in 1990. Test models are transporting passengers in Vancouver, British Columbia, and are scheduled to begin service in Chicago in mid-1997.

"Buses must continue to play a major role in urban life, but the conventional internal combustion engine cannot," Chicago Mayor Richard M. Daley said.

On May 14, 1996, Daimler-Benz, the parent company of Mercedes-Benz, unveiled a prototype of a fuel cell-powered minivan in Berlin. The **NECAR II** (New Electric Car) was an improved version of the company's first demonstration fuel-cell vehicle, introduced in 1994. **NECAR I's** fuel cell took up nearly the entire cargo area of the van, but the improved NECAR II houses the cell under its seats, leaving room for a driver and six passengers.

With some of the world's largest automakers also working to develop fuel-cell vehicles, many industry experts believe gasoline-powered cars will be replaced by the new technology. The common industry expectation is that commercial fuel-cell cars will be on the road no later than 2010.

"I've already made a bet with someone that when I turn 70 in the year 2012, I'm going to celebrate by driving a production fuel-cell vehicle," engineering editor Dennis Simanaitis of *Road & Track* magazine said at the NECAR II press conference. "None of the Daimler-Benz people want to take me up on that. There is certainty. They agree with me."

It is also likely that fuel-cell-powered cars will use **methanol** as fuel rather than pure hydrogen, which is more volatile. On-board converters will refine hydrogen from methanol, a common substance. Although the use of methanol as fuel will produce some unwanted emissions, they will be small compared to the extreme pollution caused by internal combustion engines. Since decaying garbage creates methanol as a byproduct, widespread fuel-cell use may even be helpful in addressing the problem of our ever-growing landfills.

Using hydrogen as its key element, nuclear fusion could someday provide an inexpensive and safe energy source on a large scale. Unlike fission reactions, fusion produces relatively harmless byproducts. Scientists have so far been unable to figure out how to make fusion work efficiently, because the amount of energy needed to achieve the extreme temperature required for the reaction is more than the amount of energy produced.

In 1989 American chemist **B. Stanley Pons** and British colleague **Martin Fleischmann** announced that they had managed to produce a fusion reaction at room temperature, a process known as **"cold fusion."** It appeared as if a vast new source of energy had finally been tapped, but other scientists could not duplicate and confirm the results. Cold fusion continues to elude the world's top scientists, but the quest continues for the solution to the world's energy problems.

Creation by Duplication

When scientists were initially working on the development of both nuclear fusion and fission, a major debate began, concerning the release of such awesome destructive power. A similar ethical dilemma materialized in February 1997 with the news that researchers in Scotland had successfully **"cloned"** an adult sheep. Cloning is the process of producing a replica of a specimen using the genetic code in its **DNA** (deoxyribonucleic acid), the molecules that determine an organism's unique characteristics. A team led by agricultural embryologist **Ian Wilmut** transferred cellular DNA from an adult sheep into an unfertilized egg and implanted the resulting embryo into a ewe. In July 1996 the ewe gave birth to a lamb named Dolly, an animal genetically identical to the sheep whose DNA was transferred. Scientists had previously produced clones of animals by using fetal or embryonic DNA. This process, however, only created the equivalent of identical twins rather than a genetic copy of a fully grown organism. Many experts had considered it impossible to replicate an entire adult animal.

> **"You can never plan the future by the past."**
>
> Edmund Burke

Immediately after the announcement of Wilmut's success, people began to speculate whether humans could be cloned, a concept that raised complex ethical issues. One week later, the announcement by researchers in Oregon that they had cloned two adult monkeys was convincing evidence for the possibility of human cloning, since monkeys and humans are genetically very similar.

"I certainly think it will open up the debates again and bring us back to some very old questions about what it means to be a human being and to reproduce, and the extent of the power we should have over reproduction," said Dr. Mark

The cloning of sheep opens the door for unlimited possibilities

Hanson of the Hastings Center, an ethics think tank.

Because the development was so unexpected, society as a whole is still unsure about whether human cloning should be attempted. On March 4, 1997, President Clinton prohibited federal funds to be used for such research.

"Any discovery that touches upon human creation is not simply a matter of scientific inquiry," Clinton said. "It is a matter of morality and spirituality as well."

Many scientists agree that a temporary ban on human cloning is wise in order to allow time for discussion and consideration of the ethical implications involved.

In his comments, Clinton also acknowledged the possibilities of tremendous benefits arising from cloning, such as new medical treatments, as well as highly productive livestock

strains; however, he emphasized that "like splitting the atom, this is a discovery that carries burdens as well as benefits."

With developments such as nuclear power and genetic cloning, the culmination of the technology of the 20th century places humankind in a drastically different world from the one inhabited a hundred years earlier. Utilizing their curiosity and ingenuity, humans have made monumental advances in transportation and communication, making physical distances less of an obstacle to progress. Although unexplored terrestrial territory has all but vanished, technology has opened new frontiers in outer space and cyberspace. Technology in the 21st century presents similar and new challenges, including developing improved energy sources and the ethical dilemmas of genetic cloning. In the third millennium, technology could become not only the way humans define themselves, but also the way they create themselves.

181